RELENTLESS

FORWARD

PROGRESS

RELENTLESS FORWARD PROGRESS

A Guide to Running Ultramarathons

Bryon Powell

BREAKAWAY BOOKS
HALCOTTSVILLE, NEW YORK
2011

ISBN: 978-1-891369-90-2
Library of Congress Control Number: 2011925009

Published by Breakaway Books
P.O. Box 24
Halcottsville, NY 12438
www.breakawaybooks.com

FIRST EDITION

Contents

Dedication

To all those who believed in me and gave me a second chance, thanks for letting me make Relentless Forward Progress.

Acknowledgments

I could not have written this book without the support of Meghan M. Hicks. She has been my counselor, sounding board, cheerleader, and more throughout the year and a half between this book's conception and completion. Meghan tirelessly edited each chapter (often more than once) and provided more substantive feedback than everyone else combined. I look forward to someday having the chance to edit her first book.

It's a testament to publisher Garth Battista's vision that he stuck with the idea of an ultramarathon guidebook for four years. Thanks, too, Garth, for having the faith to go with a first-time author and the patience to answer my many rookie questions. Like Garth, editor Neal Jamison was on this project from start to finish. It would not have happened without him. Eric Grossman contributed a wonderful foreword as only he could. Just as important, he's the one who brought me into the project over a casual meal during the Outdoor Retailer show two summers back. Both Neal and Eric were invaluable in guiding the book's early evolution and for providing sage advice once things got rolling.

A book is only as good as those who write it, which makes it fortunate for both you and I that so many outstanding individuals were willing to contribute their knowledge to this book. Among the experts and elites to whom I'm extremely grateful are: Adam Chase, Jamie Donaldson, William Henderson, David Horton, Dakota Jones, Karl King, Dave Mackey, Scotty Mills, Krissy Moehl, Geoff Roes, Michael Sandler, Ian Torrence, John Vonhof, and Michael Wardian. As a picture is worth a thousand words, a special thanks to PatitucciPhoto, Stephan "Gripmaster" Repke, and Glenn Tachiyama, as well as everyone who submitted a photo for consideration.

While they did so at a distance, my parents, George and Barbara Powell, and sister, Gretchen Kish, have never ceased to support me. They've been my crew for most of my 100 milers as well as for this book. I'd still be sleeping without their wake up phone calls from the East Coast to get me writing.

There are two large groups without whom I, undoubtedly, would not have written this book: my teachers and teammates. Thanks to the countless teachers who instructed me in myriad subjects. I value few things more than my liberal arts education for which I have you to thank. A special thanks to those teachers who worked with a person who fought writing at every chance. As for my teammates, clubmates, coaches, and running companions, your support and company have kept me running for the past two decades and have me looking forward to the next few decades.

Finally, a big thank you to the iRunFar community. Without all of you (as well as the counsel of Adam Chase and Garett Graubins), I wouldn't have stepped out of my professional life to write about trail and ultrarunning full time. In short, you made this book possible. Thanks!

FOREWORD

Eric Grossman

It's the middle of the night. The lantern burns with a continuous Darth Vader breath. Melinda Day hovers over her cast-iron pot, still tucked into the dying coals of her fire pit. Her children have long since eaten. She scrapes the drying bits of lasagna to combine them with the large portions remaining. Mike Day is still on the mountain.

Seven runners had gathered two days prior at Indian Grave Gap near Erwin, Tennessee. We set out to run for six days along the Appalachian Trail heading north along the Tennessee–North Carolina boarder to Grayson Highlands State Park. Our families joined us. Overnight stays were planned for campgrounds near places where the trail crossed a road after a more or less full day of running. Day 2 ended at Dennis Cove Road near Hampton, Tennessee, about a mile away from the Forest Service campground. Five of us completed the 37-mile leg in between 9 and 11 hours. One of us stopped short of the full distance and got a ride into camp. Only Mike remained on the trail.

The atmosphere of a midsummer night at a campground feels remarkably familiar. Groups of people coalesce and disperse with the quiet rhythm of mountain streams. Voices and laughter rise along with the crackle of campfires. As the fires burn down people slip away, one or two at a time, into tents or campers. The few remaining conversations combine with the insistent calls of insects and frogs to create the perfect lullaby.

Camping is a lot like running. We do it even though we don't have to. We have all the supplies we need to eat and sleep right at home. In the rare cases that we have to travel it would likely be most efficient to utilize hotels and restaurants. Instead, many of us keep a stash of sleeping bags and pads, camp pillows, propane stoves, camp cookware and utensils, lighters, coolers, and many other items that work less well than their at-home counterparts. Some of us spend weeks or months planning our camping trips. We write checklists for ourselves. We use brainpower to get properly outfitted even though the whole project is irrational.

When I prepare for camping I purposely avoid getting all the details worked out. I could rent a fully equipped RV and plan my daily itinerary online. Instead, I hastily load the van with the big things I know we need and leave the rest to the vagaries of my spotty memory. That way when I start to gather wood and realize that I forgot my ax (which nearly always happens), I am required to call upon my resources and work a little harder. Part of the appeal of camping is the challenge; making it easy and convenient would defeat the purpose.

We all contrive obstacles for ourselves. We do it so much that we sometimes forget that most (or all) of what we do is not necessary. We can justify many things we do that are beyond the minimum because we want something better for ourselves or others. We go to college so we can get a better sort of job, for example. Outdoor pursuits, and especially ultrarunning, do not fit easily into this category. We go camping, hiking, climbing, running, kayaking, and skiing even though they don't benefit us in tangible ways. These activities are tiring, risky, time consuming, and often costly. They can also be thrilling, providing experiences during which we say we feel most alive. These activities are sometimes called extreme. Running a marathon is a good challenge; running an ultramarathon demonstrates something else, something about us.

People gravitate to campfires like moths. The flames mesmerize us, dancing in tune with images from our mind's eye. Of course they do: Domesticating fire was likely a pivotal move for early humans and a vital tool for countless generations of our ancestors. The genetic instructions for building our minds were passed down from people who depended on fire for their survival. For hundreds of thousands of years our ancestors lived in small nomadic groups. Hunting or gathering during the day, they likely assembled at night around temporary shelters and, of course, fires. Camping feels familiar because our minds are designed for environments like campgrounds.

This is another surprising similarity between camping and running: It fits with our inherited dispositions. The more we learn about early humans, the more apparent it becomes that they were good at walking and running. Their quirky two-legged locomotion combined with hairlessness, sweat glands, free hands (to carry water), and vertical stature helped them manage a major problem with constant exertion—getting too hot.

Although the running habits of early humans did not preserve well in the archaeological record, we see the vestiges of our running heritage in several ancient cultures. The Japanese revere distance running. Long-distance running relays, called Ekidens, command the kind of media attention that basketball, baseball, and football do in the United States. Monastic pilgrims to Enryaku Temple near Kyoto have been dubbed the marathon monks. They set out on spiritual quests requiring between 100 and 1,000 consecutive days of running about 31 miles each day. The Tarahumara of Mexico, the San of southern Africa, aboriginal Australians, and the Masai of Kenya all have well-documented running cultures.

The Tarahumara inhabitants of the Copper Canyons in Mexico were featured in Chris McDougall's exuberant book *Born to Run*. The sense you get from the book is of a culture steeped in a run-for-its-own-sake mentality. By contrast, a short but dramatic clip from one of David Attenborough's *Life* documentaries allows you to feel the necessity of running to our early forebears. The clip shows three San tribesman of the Kalahari Desert chasing a kudu on foot—a hunt that lasts eight hours. The search term "persistence hunt" will turn up that video in many places. The same search will also turn up the hypothesis that early humans likely depended on just such hunting techniques for the tens of thousands of years that elapsed between the onset of meat eating among our ancestors and the invention of tools.

One danger of identifying people who routinely run long distances is that we will first notice the differences between them and us. They are smaller, or longer, or darker, or more ancient than us. Indeed, genetic studies of the San suggest they represent one of the most ancient African populations. And times have changed. Not even the San continue to secure food by running after kudu. While we find it easy to identify differences, commonalities often escape our notice. Like the marathon monks, many Americans run as a kind of meditation. We feel better after a stressful day of work if we spend an hour completely occupied with putting one foot in front of the other. Like the Tarahumara, we use running events as an excuse to gather. We meet in small groups for routine training runs and then we convene en masse for the occasional 5K. And some of us, like the San tribesman, set out on whole-day excursions through rough terrain. We run ultras.

Those who run long are not freaks of nature. We are not a handful of chosen ones blessed with indefatigable muscle and indestructible cartilage. Nor do we have indomitable willpower that others lack. If anything sets us apart it is a kind of sensitivity. We can hear a faint chord vibrating on old and brittle strings. It begins to resonate through us when we rise predawn for a morning run. The sound builds the longer we stay at it. On a long run through the mountains our attention becomes focused, in tune, automatic. Each footfall and each breath synchronized with a primal tune. Ours is a re-creation of once necessary dispositions.

I can still vividly recall, four years later, segments of my 37-mile run to Dennis Cove Road along the Appalachian Trail. The temperature and humidity were high, as you would expect for Tennessee in August. I carried water and snacks with a small hydration backpack. The tube for the water extended from the pack to a fastener on the strap near my chin. I started slowly. Around midday I crossed a road and began an uphill section through an overgrown field. I metered my steps, maintaining the rhythm I had established on easier sections, and clipping my strides to allow for the extra work of a hot climb. The uneven footing caused my knees to wobble slightly. I was soaked in sweat and body oil, though, so that my knees slid easily past each other. I felt like a machine, perfectly executing the task for which I had been designed.

Mike was already well behind me. He felt compelled by the invitation to run for six days through the mountains despite his chronic Achilles tendonitis. He determined to walk considerable portions of the distance each day. He knew his pace and calculated that he would finish day 2 37 miles after dark. He put "flashlight" on his packing list. His day went according to plan. He settled into position at the back of our small pack. As each of us started to establish our own pace, Mike kept to his plan, protecting his heels. It wasn't until daylight started to fade that Mike's plan unraveled. He reached into his pack for his flashlight, and it wasn't there. At first he thought that perhaps it had fallen out when he stopped to refill his water. Gradually he realized he had just forgotten to pack it. He was high on a mountain ridge. He had last crossed a road well over an hour before, and he figured that he had at least an hour left to get to Dennis Cove Road. Although he hadn't walked past any precipitous drops, he wasn't familiar with the trail and the terrain was rocky and somewhat unpredictable. He didn't want to risk continuing in the dark.

Back at camp we determined that waiting was the best option. It remained warm through the night, and we knew that the trail didn't traverse cliffs or threatening terrain. At every moment we thought that Mike would arrive the next one. We pictured him with a bad blister or strained calf limping slowly through the dim light, feeling his way along the trail. Kevin Townsend and his wife, Ann, parked their truck at the trailhead and waited. They waited all night.

At the first sign of light the rest of us prepared food and drink for Mike and for ourselves. We packed for a full day of running, and then split up the trail sections from the previous day so that we would retrace them from opposite directions. We had just convened at the trailhead for final preparations when Mike popped out of the woods. He looked well, if a bit worn. I was glad we had a few minutes to hear his story before Melinda returned from a short drive to get cell phone coverage to check for any messages from Mike. When she returned and saw her husband had safely returned, I watched only long enough to see her face melt along with all the tension she had held so stoically throughout the night.

When night had fallen and Mike realized he didn't have his flashlight, he stopped. He plopped down in the middle of the trail, drained from traversing 32 miles of rugged mountainous terrain in high heat and humidity. He finished off what bits of food he had left. Then he gave a nod to his long-gone—but not forgotten—ancestors. Long-gone because neither they nor the predators that threatened them continue to roam the woods. Not forgotten because Mike, alone and empty in the woods on top of the mountain, remained wary of the ghosts of those predators. What did he do? He gathered small pieces of wood, retrieved the matches that he had remembered to pack, and started a fire. As the flames began to lick above the scraps of collected wood, Mike curled up on the ground, bathed in the comforting glow of light and warmth.

The reassurance that Mike got from his fire is the same one that I feel when I show myself that I can run all day. While neither is necessary, both are a welcome re-creation of ancient proclivities. We are all made to feel the satisfaction of a very long run.

1

SO YOU WANT TO RUN AN ULTRAMARATHON!

What Is an Ultramarathon?

What is an ultramarathon anyway? Does it require you to run 100 miles over mountain trails in a race such as the Western States Endurance Run or to suffer through 135 road miles in the furnace-like heat of the Badwater Ultramarathon? No. Simply, an ultramarathon is any race longer than the marathon's 26 miles and 385 yards.

If you've completed a marathon and have run a few additional yards before, during, or after the race, then you've completed an ultramarathon. If you've taken a wrong turn on a long training run and, through a combination of running and walking, have covered more than 26.2 miles, then you, too, could call yourself an ultramarathoner.

Still, while both of the above scenarios technically make you an ultramarathoner, it would be somewhat disingenuous to call yourself one after such an effort. As you learn after spending time around other ultramarathoners, the sport is built upon community and the "spirit of the sport," rather than self-recognition and technicalities.

With that in mind, there's a second, implicit criterion that should be met before calling yourself an ultramarathoner: the intent to complete an ultra distance. Secondarily and with a nod to the disfavor of technicalities in ultrarunning, the intended distance should be an appreciable distance longer than the marathon. Sorry, but setting out with the aim to run 26.3 miles just doesn't sit right.

For most runners, 50-kilometer (31.1-mile) races are the gateway into "ultras," as ultramarathons are commonly known. Those seeking to test themselves with a first ultramarathon at the shorter end of the race spectrum are in luck, as the 50k distance is the most frequently raced ultra distance in most locales. To give you an idea of the prevalence of 50ks, in 2010, well in excess of 200 of them were run in the United States, while 60 were run in California alone. Other runners use time-based races of 6- or 12-hour duration to ease into the requisite distance.

To be clear, you need not run a race to have run an ultramarathon. For instance, you could meet up with a running club for an ultra-distance "fat ass" event. Traditionally, fat ass events carry some variation on the disclaimer, "No fees, no awards, no aid, no wimps." While the disclaimer may make it sound like fat ass events are no place for running a first ultra, many such events do have limited aid, and their non-competitive nature provides even more collegiality than normally found in the friendly world of ultras. If you prefer solitude, create your own first ultra, whether it involves running laps around your neighborhood or a daylong wilderness adventure run.

All that said, most runners prefer to break the ultra barrier in an official race before calling themselves ultrarunners. If you've run a marathon, you may understand the inherent feeling of accomplishment of reaching a true finish line. That feeling is repeated in your first ultra. Satisfaction lies in the act of crossing the finish line, receiving a finisher's award, and forever after being able to say, "I ran my first ultra at XYZ Race." Before race day, having a race on your calendar keeps you motivated to train when any of a countless number of detractors, from work and family, to weather and illness, threaten to derail it. At the race itself, you have a built-in supply network of aid stations, while volunteers, spectators, and fellow competitors aid you in your journey beyond the marathon.

Why Run an Ultramarathon?*

You may still be considering whether or not you want to train for an ultra—or perhaps you're looking for some reassurance for continuing to do so. While it is unlikely that training for and racing an ultramarathon will be easy throughout, there are many reasons to run an ultra, whether it's your 1st or 40th.

For starters, if this will be your first ultramarathon, you will experience a journey into the unknown. The ultramarathon represents a new challenge in attempting to run farther than you ever have before. Rest assured that the challenge is both physical and mental. Find out if you have what it takes.

The complicated and unpredictable nature of ultramarathons can, somewhat counterintuitively, help you reconnect with running. Devon Crosby-Helms, winner of the 2008 Vermont 100-miler, suggests,

Training for and running an ultramarathon is something
to get excited about. (Photo by PatitucciPhoto.com)

* This section is adapted from the article "It's Time to Run Your First Ultramarathon!," which originally appeared on Running.Competitor.com.

"A good reason to switch from marathons [to ultras] is because in ultras you have to think about more than just splits and ticking off miles at a certain pace. I think it reconnects you with running in a way that marathoning doesn't."

Training for and racing ultramarathons also connects you with a new group of friends. Most folks who have crossed over from sub-ultradistance road racing have found a tight-knit but welcoming community. Ultrarunners are often eager to share the trail with anyone dipping his or her toe into the ultra world. Not only are these runners welcoming, they are an invaluable resource. Coach Lisa Smith-Batchen suggests to new ultrarunners, "Find a group of people that are already running on the trails so they can help you." Likewise, if you're training for a road ultra, find some folks training for one. Don't worry if you're already active in a running club or community; many ultrarunners enjoy the company of multiple running groups. Variety is the spice of life, after all!

American runners spend the vast majority of their running miles pounding the pavement. On the other hand, most North American ultramarathons are run on trails, so getting ready for one is a great excuse to get off the pavement and up into the hills. While you're up there you might just see spectacular things. Scotty Mills, who has run ultras for more than a quarter century, notes, "The advantages of training for trail ultras over road marathons are the beauty of the trails, the shared trail time in remote areas, and the peaceful feeling of training with the mind-set that you can run forever."

Running an ultra also provides a great break from competitive pressures, while still giving you a goal to shoot for. It's easy to get caught up in racing when there are 10,000 runners blasting down the course with you. The smaller fields, longer distances, and variable conditions of ultras help shift your competition from others to yourself. Knowing that others are thinking the same way makes this transition all the easier. Plus, if it's your first ultra, you'll set a PR no matter how long it takes you to finish! Finally, as Mills points out,

"The training and friends you make in ultrarunning are the real pay-offs; the race itself can almost be secondary in importance."

In attempting to do what so few people have done, you may end up inspiring yourself. "The mind is a very powerful thing, and it's generally the only thing standing between you and something incredible. You can always do more than you think you can," suggests ultra-convert Paige Troelstrup. In a similar vein, Leadville Trail 100-mile founder Ken Choulber is often heard reminding runners, "You're tougher than you think you are, and you can do more than you think you can." Go find out if Ken is right!

How to Use This Book to Run an Ultramarathon

Whatever your reasons, you've come to this book in search of guidance for running an ultramarathon, perhaps your first—and that is what you'll find. This book begins by providing a basic framework for ultramarathon training. Following this foundation, you will find training plans for 50ks (31 miles), moderate-distance ultras of 40 miles to 100k (62 miles), and longer ultras of 100 miles and beyond. You'll also receive a concise education on trail running, a vital component of most ultramarathons.

You'll learn many lessons en route to a successful ultramarathon. These lessons can be slowly and sometimes painfully self-taught through trial and error. This books aims to shorten the learning process and minimize unneeded suffering by instructing you regarding the ins and outs of ultramarathon hydration and nutrition. Even if you consume the correct fluid and fuel to keep you going on the course, injuries and other challenges can be a quick way to a DNF (did not finish), so they are covered, too. You'll also want the right gear while training and racing, so that's covered, as well.

Once you have the tools and training, it's time to attempt your first ultramarathon. Learn how to prepare for race day and how to approach the race itself. In general, the nutrition, required gear, pacing, environmental conditions, and time on your feet for an ultra differ significantly even from a marathon. In fact, environmental conditions, from blistering heat to breath-stealing altitude, are encountered often enough in ultras to warrant a chapter of their own.

Last but not least, this book offers a few options for exploring and then expanding the world of ultramarathons. Ultras are a social phenomenon; chapter 14 touches on various ways for sharing your journey with others, and points out community-based resources. Finally, the afterword examines variations on the ultramarathon theme, including adventure runs, endurance snowshoeing, fast-packing, and stage races.

Ultrarunning elites and subject area experts have weighed in with their advice to help round out the pages of this book. The widely varying contributions are presented in each runner's own voice from Krissy Moehl's inspirational essay on why you should run an ultra to Karl King's technical insight on hydration and electrolyte balance and from David Horton's decades-long perspective on how to pre-pare for your first ultra to Dakota Jones' fresh take on trail steward-ship. I trust you will find their thoughts as valuable as I have.

Why Run an Ultra?

Krissy Moehl

Why run an ultra? Because you are looking for that next challenge? Because you have recently met someone who runs farther on their "training" runs than you would consider even racing and you saw that sparkle in their eyes when they spoke of the trails and the mountains?

How often in life do we have the opportunity to inspire ourselves? Often we look outward, to other individuals and teams, to fill that need for inspiration, whether it be in our work, sport, or daily living. Pushing your physical limits, putting yourself to an unknown challenge is personally inspiring.

It inspires you to get out of bed in the morning and train no matter the weather. It inspires you to learn more about nutrition, training, and equipment to help you accomplish the task. To make it to the starting line is personal inspiration and to pull off the feat is an accomplishment hard to match. You know the time you have dedicated to that end goal, to the finish line. You know the experiences you've gained through the process as well as the tough times you endured to make it happen. It is a very personal goal and one that will fulfill a soul.

The energy gained in having a goal, in training for that goal, and reaching that achievement not only grounds your daily life, but also adds meaning and purpose. It creates memories both personal and shared. It brings you into a community no matter where you travel, because runners like you exist all over the world.

I am lucky (I think) to say that my first experiences on the trails were guided by our sport's greats. They knew I would be a quick convert when, rather than making the comment, "I don't like to drive my car 100 miles," upon learning of Scott Jurek's first Western States win, I instead inquired more about trail running. "What do you eat? When do you use the bathroom? Where do I sign up?"

Since then and with guidance, I found the answers to those questions. I have been fortunate to compete healthfully for the last 10 years in distances ranging from 50k to 100 miles. Most of those races were run on some of the most beautiful trails around the world. I have enjoyed the highs and lows that come through these intense experiences and seem to find balance with it as the years go by.

Each race offers its own experience, story, and lasting life change, so it is difficult to pick my best race experience. If forced, two come to mind. The first is my 2007 win and course record at the Hardrock 100. That year, Scott Jurek, the mentor who got me into the sport and who has become like a big brother since, won the men's division. Standing on the Hardrock with Scott in Silverton, the race's finish line, was an incredibly meaningful and exhilarating moment after challenging myself through Colorado's San Juan Mountains.

In 2009 I returned to the Ultra-Trail du Mont-Blanc. Returned? I was fortunate to spend a couple of weeks in France in 2003 and run the first edition of UTMB. That year the weather was horrendous, and those who finished the full tour around the Mont Blanc massif were few. It was my longest race to that point, 155 kilometers (93 miles), and with the weather and a strained IT band reducing me to a walk for the last 30 miles, it remains my most challenging run—one where I learned about perseverance paying off as I won the race.

To return in 2009 was an absolute treat! I stood on the starting line with 2,500 runners; it was the largest ultra field I have ever competed with, and definitely the most incredible group of spectators. The crowds were impressive into the night, with bands playing and the streets lined with people sharing high-fives and cheering us on. Traversing the ridges in the wee hours of the morning and listening to the cowbells in the distance provided the opportunity to gather inspiration from within, to dig deep, to push through the sleepiness that ensues with darkness, and to find motivation in the simple process of putting one foot in front of the other.

My opportunity to really see what I was capable of came at the 110k mark, where I moved into first position for women. With 55k to go, I challenged myself to run those final miles harder than any 50k race I had run before. This was no small feat considering the three major climbs ahead. Cresting the final climb, giving everything to the final descent into Chamonix, and ignoring the pain in my patella tendons literally brought tears of joy. The feeling of flying (at least it felt like it to me) in to the Ultra-Trail du Mont-Blanc finish line, where the streets were lined with people cheering, and crossing under that finish line into the arms and support of the people who were with me throughout the event was not only extraordinary, but life changing. It was an incredible crowning moment that summarized a year of personal preparation, a night and day of running to the best of my ability, and, most important, community.

I like to say that if you hang around me long enough, I'll get you to run an ultra. This energy actually applies to most ultra-runners. Once you have tried the challenge of running on the trails and fallen in love with the feeling of the trees whipping by, the incredible views you are able to gain in a morning run, and the laughs you've shared in the middle of nowhere with fellow ultrarunners, there really is no going back; you are personally inspired. As you talk about experiences you find that your speech quickens and your eyes sparkle. That energy transfers to those around you, and soon more ultrarunners are born.

Krissy Moehl (visor) savoring having won the
2009 Ultra-Trail du Mont-Blanc. (Photo by Sho Fujimaki)

Krissy Moehl is a race director, coach, and one of ultrarunning's finest ambassadors. She's twice won the Ultra-Trail du Mont-Blanc ('03 and '09) as well as the Hardrock 100 ('07), Wasatch 100 ('04), and many other ultramarathons.

2

THE BUILDING BLOCKS OF ULTRAMARATHON TRAINING

This chapter discusses the major elements of ultramarathon training. You'll first learn about the importance of training volume and long runs as well as how to incorporate back-to-back long runs and speed work into your training. Ultra training isn't always about doing more, so recovery and burnout are discussed at length. Finally, the chapter concludes with a look at why you might want to consider working with a coach as you prepare for an ultra.

Turn Up the Training Volume

There is perhaps no better predictor of ultramarathon success than total training volume. Make consistent, significant mileage a primary goal throughout your ultramarathon training along with logging your long runs. You don't want to overdo it, but one of the best ways to run better at any race length, and especially in ultras, is to run more.

The good news regarding weekly mileage, however, is that you'll be fine whatever your weekly mileage is so long as you get your long runs in. Really. You can complete an ultra and do so with great success without logging more miles on your feet than you do in your car.

Training Pace

Before diving into the details of how much you should be running, there's the critical or, as it turns out, not so critical factor in your day-to-day training—your standard training pace. My advice? Run comfortably. With the exception of a steep hill here or there, there is no excuse for not being able to talk continually during the vast majority of your training. Unless you are running a road 50k, your average race day pace will likely be slower than your training pace. If you're a competitve runner or a driven personality, it's more likely that you are running too fast during your training runs than too slow.

Weekly Mileage

On the low-mileage end, it would be beneficial, or at least make for a better experience, if you were running at least 35 to 40 miles per week before attempting an ultramarathon. Regular weekly tallies around 50 miles often lead to strong, comfortable ultra finishes. If you log upward of eight weeks near 70 miles per week, you'll be in top form and, if you've had success at other distances, will likely be competitive at many ultras. As for running 100 miles or more per week, very few ultrarunners do so, and many of them are the very best in the sport.

If you're an experienced distance runner—that is, someone who's consistently trained for at least a few years—and you've recently trained for a marathon, aim to run at least as many miles per week in your peak ultramarathon training as you did in your peak marathon training. Likewise, other weeks in your training program should be similar to or slightly higher than their corresponding weeks in your marathon-training schedule.

If you're a newer runner, if you have bumped up to the marathon distance in the past year, or if you've been relatively injury-free at a mileage plateau for a few years, it might now be the time to increase your mileage by 10 miles per week during your peak training.

It can be tempting to attempt a massive jump in overall training volume from one season* to the next. Such a jump is risky and ill

* By a season, I mean five or six months of training followed by a rest period.

advised. Instead, take a long view in which you sequentially increase mileage over multiple seasons. While I can't offer a hard-and-fast rule, I wouldn't advise an experienced runner to increase his or her season-over-season volume by much more than 20 percent. That means a 50-mile-per-week runner could bump up to 60 miles per week, and a 70-mile-per-week runner could target 85 miles per week. Newer runners who have logged 40 or fewer miles per week in previous seasons may be able to increase their mileage more dramatically on a percentage basis. It's not uncommon for a rapidly improving, less experienced runner to increase his or her mileage by 10 or even 20 miles per week from one season to the next.

Increasing Weekly Mileage and the 10 Percent Rule

Whether you make a concerted effort to up your weekly mileage or it comes naturally through exciting, injury-free training, sudden jumps in weekly mileage are a bad idea. They often manifest in injury or training burnout. Focus on making relentless forward progress in training rather than looking for leaps up followed by hard crash landings. Even experienced runners need to remind themselves (or sometimes be reminded by those around them) to aim for a slow, steady progression. It means very little if you are feeling great a week or two after a big jump in mileage, as you may end up paying your dues with an injury a week later or burned out a few weeks before your big race.

You've likely heard of the "10 Percent Rule" for increasing your mileage. If not, it suggests that you increase your weekly mileage by no more than 10 percent week-to-week. In general, it's a great rule to follow. However, there are exceptions. For instance, most experienced runners amp up their mileage faster than 10 percent a week after a rest period—and that's fine. That said, the smart ones apply the principle behind the rule, which is to increase your mileage only in considered, reasonable amounts.

You, too, should apply the 10 Percent Rule more as a guideline than as a commandment. That's not a ticket to add 15 miles to your total mileage week after week. Instead, it's a call to recognize the arbitrary nature of what constitutes a training week, the arbitrary nature of the rule being exactly 10 percent, and the increased irregularity of weekly mileage in ultramarathon training.

In analyzing increases in your training volume, look beyond your Monday-to-Sunday or Sunday-to-Saturday week. While there is no need to scrutinize every possible seven-day period, keep the possibility of other periods of far-too-quick mileage increase in mind.

For instance, let's say you've been running 45 to 50 miles per week. After taking a few days off from Monday though Wednesday, you end up running 40 miles from Thursday through Sunday. You then kick off the following week with 30 miles from Monday through Wednesday. Regardless of what you plan for the remainder of the second week, with 70 miles in seven days, you likely ran too much in too short a period. There's no need to panic. Simply ease back your training volume by 10 to 15 percent below your established mileage (here, 45 to 50 miles per week) for the following seven days.

More frequent and longer long runs and even the occasional set of back-to-back long runs make your weekly mileage jump around a bit more than during training for a road marathon. Consider keeping a secondary, longer-term measure of training volume, such as a three-week moving average of weekly volume. Such measures are useful not only for warning of short-term overuse and possible resultant injuries, but also as a hedge against cumulative fatigue that can lead to burnout.

The 10 Percent Rule and a regular look at a mileage moving average are useful tools. However, the broad message to remember is that, despite their utility, logging massive miles should not be done at the expense of your physical or mental health. If you need to take a few days off to heal from a minor injury or illness, do so. If the combination of your training and other obligations has you on the brink of collapse, analyze all your obligations and determine which need to be pared. If that includes cutting your weekly mileage by 10 or 20 miles for a week or two, but being better rested, less stressed, and happier, then you and your running might very well benefit in the long term from a short recovery period. Take care of yourself and make relentless forward progress.

On the Long Run

While total training volume may be the best predictor of ultra-marathon success, it is paramount that you include long runs in your ultra training. In fact, it's often better to sacrifice a small amount of training volume in the form of pre- and post-long-run recovery to ensure that you can make the most of your long runs. Similarly, curtail speed work and other intense training as needed to make sure that you can make it through your long runs. You don't need to log a long run every week, but as a general rule, the more long runs, the better.

If you've run one or two marathons, start building up your long runs from shorter distances. Progressively increase that distance more slowly than someone who has cranked out a multiple marathons every year for a few years.

Many marathon programs call for long runs every other week. As you build toward an ultra, try to get in long efforts most weeks. In transitioning to doing so, alternate between shorter and longer long runs to provide relative breaks on a regular basis.

Do not become scared by the numbers that follow. They are a guide for those looking at a long-term buildup prior to running various ultra distances. If you are training for a 50k, log a few runs of around 25 miles with as many 18- to 22-mile runs as you feel comfortable with. For a 50-miler, hit 25 or so miles a couple of times with maybe one effort of around 30 miles. An easy way to log the 30-miler is to run a 50k race as that long run.

Don't run a 100-mile race as your first ultra. Why? Not because it's impossible, but because your experience is likely to be more pleasant and your chances of finishing higher if you first run a few other ultras. In particular, shoot for running at least one 50k and either a 50-mile or a 100-kilometer event as part of your buildup to the 100-miler. Alternatively, if you want to be an ultramarathon race virgin when you hit the 100-mile starting line, your training might include numerous 20- to 30-mile runs, one in the 30-to-35-mile range, and a 40-to-50-mile run.

In advance of any focus ultramarathon, plan on running two or three tune-up races in which you test your gear, nutrition plan, and fitness. It's perfectly acceptable to run additional races as your long runs, so long as you complete the events without competing. Think of these noncompetitive races as supported long runs with added fans and companions. Do not get in the habit of pushing yourself to complete exhaustion in these "non-races." If you do, you'll be cutting into your weekday training too often while also increasing your risk of injury and fatigue.

As will be discussed in chapter 3, specificity is a key aspect of ultramarathon training. You should log at least a few long runs in conditions that mimic those you're likely to encounter on race day. It's important to match the running surface (road, trail, or trail with very poor footing) and topography of the race (flat, hilly, or mountainous). Similarly, while there's nothing wrong with pushing the pace during an occasional long run, it's critical that some of your long runs mirror the slower pace to be expected during your ultra. Your running gait changes along with your pace, so you'll want to be comfortable and trained to run slower than what feels right for a fresh five mile run around town.

Training on mountainous trails prepares you for racing on mountainous trails.   (Photo by Glenn Tachiyama)

Put Your Back into It: Back-to-Back Long Runs

Some ultrarunners swear by back-to-back (B2B) long training runs. They hypothesize that it's necessary to learn how to run on tired legs. However, regularly running a significant portion of your weekly miles on tired legs is asking for injury. Instead, consider using B2Bs judiciously in your ultramarathon training.

For instance, benefits exist in strategically running a B2B three to six weeks before an ultra, especially your first. It's great to have some experience in dealing with heavy, unresponsive legs as well as with a beat-up psyche in advance of race day. There are, of course, the benefits inherent to running extra miles, especially long-run miles. If spaced out with adequate recovery, running two or even three B2Bs in the season leading up to your focus ultra is beneficial.

If you do run one or more B2Bs, be hypervigilant with regard to injury on the second day and in subsequent days. Don't confuse acute injury-related pain with fatigue or muscle soreness, which is what you are learning to deal with on these runs. Be sure to give yourself adequate recovery following any B2Bs.

If, when planning a B2B, you decide to run one hillier route, such as on mountain trails that will require intermittent hiking, and one entirely runnable effort, schedule the runnable session first. You will have no problem walking up steep climbs and rolling down hills on road-deadened legs, but you aren't very likely to enjoy running for hours straight with an unchanging gait on already tired legs.

Back-to-back runs can also useful in advanced ultra training. An experienced ultrarunner may head out for massive B2B or even a back-to-back-to-back long weekend shortly before tapering into a big race. This final training push might be as much as 100 miles over a three-day period.

Bonk Runs

A number of elite ultrarunners use an advanced B2B technique known to some as the "bonk run." On day 1 of this B2B, you complete a moderate-to-high-intensity run of at least 25 miles, but up to 35 miles. While hydration and electrolyte consumption remain important, you don't consume any calories during or in the few hours following the run. The point of the first run is to deplete your muscle glycogen stores. The second run is a more modestly paced run in the 20-to-25-mile range. Again, you abstain from consuming any calories during this second run and don't compensate by having a large, carbohydrate-rich meal beforehand. The more depleted you can keep your glycogen levels for this second run, the better. You are quite likely to feel lethargic, cranky, or downright miserable from late in the first run until you eat after the second run. That's all part of the process.

The Need for Speed:
Intervals, Fartleks, and Tempo Runs, Oh My!

Many runners who have followed a marathon-training program or who have trained to competitively run shorter-distance races are familiar with the concept of speed work. Speed work includes various training tools like fartleks, hill repeats, tempo runs, and intervals. Speed work has many purposes depending on how it's structured. Benefits range from improved running efficiency and injury prevention to increased speed and enhanced fat metabolism.

Speed work is exhilarating. (Photo by PatitucciPhoto.com)

There are multiple schools of thought regarding the need for speed work during ultramarathon training. Dueling essays regarding the need for speed from Ian Torrence (pro) and Geoff Roes (con) explore both sides of the debate. This book takes the position that speed work is an unnecessary but welcome component. With that in mind, speed work is included in the training plans found in sub-

sequent chapters with explanations of alternative, non-speed workouts. However, if you have never run speed work or have found
yourself prone to injury when you have included speed work in your
training regimen, ease into it with care. Ratchet back the intensity
of workouts if you're uncomfortable with moving at the prescribed
speed. On the other hand, if you are comfortable with the speed, but
haven't recently run at similar speeds for close to the prescribed distance, run the set intensity while gradually building up the total volume of speed work in a given session. If you feel strongly that any
speed work presents too great a risk of injury, then substitute a continuous run equal to the day's prescribed mileage, with the bulk of
the run at the fastest pace you are comfortable running.

There are a slew of speed work options, each with its very specific
benefits. Choosing a precise mix of speed work at very specific paces
is important for shorter races as well as elite ultramarathoners aim-
ing for unfathomably quick road ultra times. For the rest of us, I
feel that the devil isn't in the details; rather, it's more likely to be in
worrying about the details. I would, instead, categorize speed work
into two broad categories, interval and tempo work, with striders
being a tool that falls outside the scope of speed work.

For purposes of this book, intervals incorporate a range of workouts that consist of 2 to 5 miles of high-intensity running interspersed
with breaks. These workouts are run near a runner's maximum aerobic capacity (VO_2 max). Most reminiscent of high school or college
track are pure intervals. These workouts are uncomfortable, anaerobic or near-anaerobic efforts usually of one to five minutes each with
recovery times ranging from half to the full length of the interval.
These intervals could be run on a track, road, or non-technical trail
and be based on either time or distance. Long hill repeats on gradual
climbs with interval and recovery lengths on par with those just
described also fall into this category. Fartleks, or fun runs, are less
structured speed workouts containing pickups based on terrain or
landmarks or set at nearly random intervals. While the effort, length,

and total volume of the pickups as well as the recovery fall into the range of pure intervals, the less structured nature of fartleks can make them less intimidating and more enjoyable.

Tempo runs are runs performed near or at your lactate threshold. For most runners, lactate threshold pace is approximately the pace you could hold for one hour of racing. The purpose of the tempo run is not to go all-out, but to evenly maintain lactate threshold pace throughout the workout, which typically lasts 20 to 40 minutes after a 15-to-20-minute warm-up. Cruise intervals or LT intervals are one alternative to tempo runs. Cruise intervals involve 3-to-10-minute tempo efforts with a 30-to-60-second recovery jog. Cumulative time at tempo effort should be the same or slightly higher for cruise intervals than in standard tempo runs.

A small number of ultrarunners may do 8 to 12 "strides" at the end of two or three runs each week. Strides are short 80-to-120-meter sprints at a "fast but relaxed" effort with plenty of recovery; they're aimed at improving running economy rather than cardiovascular conditioning. Build up your speed gradually over 70 meters while concentrating on staying relaxed with good form before holding your speed through the end of the stride.

Traditionally, speed work consisting of efforts less than a minute, whether on the track or as short hill repeats, has been thought to have only tangential utility in ultras in that they are useful for building leg strength and improving running economy. Some emerging research suggests that high-intensity interval training, such as 8 x 20 seconds all-out with 10 seconds' rest, may significantly improve VO_2 max, a prime indicator of endurance performance. However, it's my opinion that an experienced marathoner looking to complete his or first ultra would be best served by concentrating on longer speed workouts.

A number of ultrarunning coaches whom I deeply respect place much more emphasis on highly structured training. Including a more purposeful and regimented speed work routine is a perfectly valid approach to ultramarathon training. If you routinely join others for speed work, your coach prescribes it, you enjoy having it in your routine, or you're attempting to maintain your speed for sub-ultra races during or after your ultramarathon training, do not let this section dissuade you from continuing to do so. I merely suggest not emphasizing speed work to the point that it limits your ability to log long runs.

Even those who shy away from traditional speed work would benefit from including some intensity into their training. Intensity can be found in countless places. You might head out for a short local road or trail race every few weeks. Maybe you meet up once a week with a training partner who's a good deal faster than you are. I like running up many-mile-long gradual, continuous hills at a steady effort. Intensity need not even come from running. Walking quickly up a steep climb or even going for a snowshoe session in some powder can really get your heart pounding and muscles moving without feeling like speed work.

The Need for Speed?: Why Speed Training Is Unnecessary for Ultramarathons

Geoff Roes

Recently, I ran about 1 mile fast. I don't run fast in my training very often, but usually in the 10 days or so before races I do some short tempo stuff to keep my legs turning over as I rest more and more to get ready for a race.

Running fast for a bit got me thinking about speed training and raw speed capability and how or if they apply much at all to ultra running success. I was thinking of the upcoming The North Face Endurance Challenge 50 mile championships and was wondering if the eventual winner of the race would finish in the top 10 if the race were a 10k instead of 50 miles?—or even a marathon compared with 50 miles. In each of these examples, I am fairly certain there would be a huge shake-up in where various front of the pack runners would finish.

The interesting question to me is: Why is this the case? Does each runner have a certain distance or style of running (flat, hilly, technical, et cetera) that they naturally excel at, or do certain runners do a better job of figuring out how to adapt to a certain distance or style of running? I guess in reality it's probably a little bit of both. I've known more than a few runners who would say it's almost entirely the former reason; the latter has almost no relevance. I disagree strongly. I think the reason there are dozens of sub-2:30 marathoners out there who have had a hard time finding their groove in 50- and 100-mile trail races isn't simply because they aren't suited for longer distances, but more because they have too much of an idea of how to train for running marathons. That is to say that they get caught up thinking that training for a 50- or 100-miler is quite similar to training for a marathon. A handful of fast marathoners have been able to fake it up to 50 miles, but for every one of these there are several who get to mile 30 or 35 in their first 50 and are completely fried. At that point all the leg speed in the world ain't gonna do much of anything for you.

How, then, do you prepare your body (and mind) to race well for a full 50 or 100 miles? There are a lot of potential answers to this question, but, in my mind, the most important one is to let go of the idea that we need to focus in our training on improving our leg speed. Racing 50 or 100 miles is about strength and endurance. It's about nutrition and hydration. It's about patience, stubbornness, and determination. It's about a lot of things, but it's really not much about leg speed. Sure, there are great ultrarunners with great shorter-distance speed, but there are also great ultrarunners with mediocre (at best) shorter-distance speed. The fact that two-time Leadville 100-mile champion Anton Krupicka's 5k PR is about 16:30 should be all the proof we need on this point. In nearly every ultra he runs he beats dozens of runners who would beat him if the race were a 5k. Why? Take a look at his training. He runs a ton and he runs uphill on rugged trails. He does more in training to build his strength and endurance than anyone I've ever heard of. And, more important, he does more or less nothing in his training to build his leg speed.

Take me as another example. I'm blessed with a bit more leg speed than Tony, but it was when I stopped thinking that I needed to try to sharpen and hone this leg speed that I began to have the high level of success in ultras that I had in late 2009 through 2010.

This isn't to say that you can't be successful at ultras if you do speed work in your training, but I do believe that doing speed work in training for 50- and 100-mile races (especially hilly, technical ones) does nothing to make us "faster" on race day, and in most cases probably makes us slower because it uses up time and energy in training that could be better spent increasing our strength and endurance.

This reminds me of a recent run with some friends here in Colorado. As we climbed, the snow got pretty deep. Eventually we were just trudging through knee-deep snow as we headed higher and higher into the mountains. It was a fun group of runners, and no one was complaining about the conditions. However, I remember elite ultrarunner Dakota Jones saying that although he was enjoying the hike up through the snow, he didn't really imagine that any of this was going to be very beneficial come The North Face championships where he and I would both be racing. Well, Dakota was nineteen (a very wise nineteen) then, and I'm sure he'll figure out soon enough the value in the strength and endurance one builds from moving uphill, at a steady pace, through knee deep snow. Luckily for me, most strong runners who come from a road marathon background never take the time or have the patience to figure this out.

Geoff Roes is an elite ultramarathoner who shattered the Western States 100 course record in 2010 with a time of 15:07:04. He's twice won Ultrarunning *magazine's Men's Ultrarunner of the Year award ('09 and '10) and has won each of his first seven 100-mile races. This essay is adapted from an article Geoff first published on his blog found at AKRunning.blogspot.com.*

Racing Far Is No Excuse for Training Slow

Ian Torrence

If you never run fast, you'll never run fast.
—Bernie Boettcher, four-time Pikes Peak Marathon
and Ascent masters winner

By definition, ultrarunners are proficient at running long and relatively slow. However, this necessary practice of time-consuming long-distance training has, for many, become an accepted reason to avoid another important facet of competitive ultrarunning: speed training. Why should runners who participate in 24-plus-hour long races with seemingly pedestrian-like course records equivalent to a 9-, 10-, or 11-minute-per-mile average pace incorporate speed work into their training?

Nikki Kimball, winner of the 2004 Western States 100 Mile Endurance Run and three-time winner of the USA Track and Field 50 Mile Trail Championships, credits her rise to elite status to the introduction of speed work into her training regimen. "Starting my ultra career in New England, where the trails are actually technical, speed training seemed, at first, a little silly. However, even the most techy trail races have long sections of eminently runnable sections on which one needs leg speed in order to place well."

Though uncomfortable, the goal of speed work is to spend time at your maximum aerobic capacity (or VO_2 max). Training at this effort level improves the body's ability to work harder for a longer period of time. Typically, this is achieved by running 400-to-2000-meter intervals or repeats at 2-to-5-mile race pace with a recovery jog of either half the distance or approximately half the time of the fast interval. The recovery jogs help you maintain the prescribed speed for the entire training run.

Greg McMillan, an exercise physiologist and coach for McMillan Elite and Team USA Arizona, explains the physiological benefits of speed work on his coaching website McMillanRunning.com. "While endurance (slow, easy running) and stamina (8-to-30-kilometer race pace running) training stimulate adaptations that improve the efficiency of several systems of the body, speed training works to actually increase the capacity of several of your body's systems. Research shows that speed training increases the enzymes that help liberate energy from our fuel sources, improves the lactic acid buffering capacity, provides a greater stimulation and training of the fast-twitch muscle fibers, and results in a greater ability to extract oxygen from the blood as it perfuses the muscles."

In the January–February 2010 edition of *Running Times,* Jim Gerweck makes the case that repetitive stress, or doing the same thing every day, like running long, slow distance, can lead to overuse injuries. Gerweck quotes Terrence Mahon, coach of the Mammoth Track Club: "The body gets really good at doing what you ask it to, and becomes more efficient at it. So if you hit it with the same stressors season after season, you begin to get less and less training response. You can't do the same thing you did the year before and expect to improve if you've been running for a while. You've got to add different elements of stress."

Runners of all levels must challenge themselves during training if they wish to maximize their performance on race day. Dave Dunham, ultrarunner and team manager for the Teva US Mountain Running Junior Team, states, "The main reason for speed training is that slow running just makes you run slow! It is important to mix things up to avoid staleness. Nothing shakes up your training like a good hard track workout. Speed work is a great indicator of your fitness level."

Other benefits of speed training include increasing training intensity without risking burnout or overtraining, improving range of motion, and developing adeptness at traveling over rugged, technical trails. Howard Nippert, coach and USA Track and Field 100-kilometer national champion, adds, "Running slow distance all the time or hills for strength never allows you to open your stride and develop strength through a full range of motion. You have to do some fast running in order to open your stride. Should you encounter uneven or technical footing, the ability to pick your feet up and put them down quickly is beneficial to moving through that style of terrain."

Psychological benefits of speed work include the development of mental resilience and an improved awareness of your ability to maintain varying paces at different distances. Dave Mackey, who set course records at California's 2010 Dick Collins Firetrails 50 Mile and the 2011 USA Track and Field 100 Kilometer Trail Championships in Texas, thinks that speed work may provide you the confidence you need to break out of a racing rut. "If your body already has an immense base of miles and can finish an ultra without too much trouble, then the next step is to incorporate some speed to help finish that ultra even faster."

Like Mackey, Bernie Boettcher agrees that toughening bouts of fast training can come in handy while trying to break through on race day. "In a long, hard trail race, this speed work helps steel my resolve when faced with the agonies of screaming muscles. In my mind, I can tell myself, *This ain't nuthin' yet,* and keep pushing."

Many ultrarunners escape to the trails because they do not enjoy the speed training associated with road and track running. Speed work can be disguised in many ways and doesn't have to be done on a track or a treadmill. Try speed play on your next trail run; attack both the uphills and downhills or chase a friend who's just a bit faster than you are. Take Mackey's suggestion when thinking about incorporating speed work into your training: "At the very least, it sure won't hurt you and you may have a good time doing it if you design it right, like on flat dirt versus a boring track."

Ian Torrence has completed 155 ultras, including 24 100-mile races and the Grand Slam of Ultrarunning. He works in Flagstaff, Arizona, as an ultramarathon online coach at McMillanRunning.com. He has written for Running Times, Ultrarunning, Marathon & Beyond, *and currently contributes to* Running Times *Trails Online.*

Recovery

If overall training volume is so valuable to an ultrarunner, then it follows that those things that keep you training consistently throughout the lead-up to your focus race are equally valuable. Enter recovery as a key element of your training program. It's an element upon which ultrarunners focus on a daily, monthly, and yearly basis.

The occasional B2B notwithstanding, the standard approach of alternating hard and easy days stands true in ultra training. After nearly every hard effort, be it speed work, a focused hill session, or a long run, follow it with an easy day.

For most runners, easy days include low-volume, low-intensity runs as well as one or two run-free days each week. Easy runs should be easy. If you can't converse for the entire run, slow down! On your easy days, aim to run between 50 to 75 percent of the volume you run during other weekday runs.

If, through your running history, you've found that your body cannot handle running more than four days per week, you can still run an ultra. Timing permitting, consider incorporating one or two moderate cross-training sessions per week.

High-intensity or high-volume cross-training days are not full rest days. On the other hand, a light cross-training session of an hour or less is active recovery. Active recovery consists of an alternative sport, such as a swim, a mountain bike ride, or even an easy walk in the evening. Keep in mind that the main purpose of active recovery is to recover and not to get in additional training. Active recovery is especially useful in the day or days following an intense or difficult long run.

The greatest single exception to a regular on–off pattern is one of convenience. For many, weekday running is constrained by time. We are constantly barraged by obligations. We're faced with work, family, school, errands, and countless other demands. The timing of many of these demands is out of our control, and we are left to squeeze in our runs whenever we can. These scheduled demands are often greatest during the week, which leaves the weekend relatively open for running. It's hard not to want to take advantage of weekend's flexibility, so the training plans in this book embrace it.

In fact, the weekend's openness is likely a key reason for the popularity of B2B weekend long runs week in and week out. It's a matter of convenience. There is, however, a happy middle ground between constant B2Bs and "wasting" one weekend day. On whichever day isn't your long run, head out for an easy-effort run of approximately the same length or marginally longer than your "on" weekday runs. For example, if you typically run 8 to 10 miles on Tuesday and Thursday, follow a Saturday long run with an easy 8 to 12 miles on Sunday, with Monday being an easy day.

Even if you faithfully alternate between hard and easy days, your body will need more significant breaks as you gradually build your training volume and intensity. When you step up your weekly training volume, hold it at a given level for two to three weeks before easing off the volume by 15 to 20 percent for a week. After this rest week, take another step up in your weekly training volume during the next training period.

Because this book errs on the side of caution in favor of maintaining consistent, injury-free progress, the included training schedules are based on no more than three up weeks followed by one recovery week. As training volume and intensity increase, recovery weeks are scheduled every third week or even more frequently. Should your running or life schedule dictate the occasional three-week up period later in the training plan, don't worry about it so long as you feel recovered as you begin the next up period.

Making relentless forward progress as an ultrarunner (or an ultra-hopeful in training) involves regularly easing off the accelerator. That holds true even after a training season, and not just for new ultra-runners. Many of the sport's elite take a significant break from running after their competitive season is complete. For example, seven-time Western States 100 winner Scott Jurek has taken four to six weeks completely off from running at the end of a number of his racing seasons. Similarly, Kilian Jornet, a two-time winner of the 103-mile Ultra-Trail du Mont-Blanc, rarely runs between November and April. However, he remains quite active. You see, he's a world champion ski mountaineer. His change of sports reduces the cumulative pounding on his joints even as he maintains his fitness on the snow. You, too, should consider scheduling official post-focus ultra breaks in which you either don't run at all, or significantly reduce your mileage and run only for fun. In doing so, you will recharge your body and your mind.

Tips for Recovery

Adequate recovery on a day-to-day basis can be the difference between an all-right training season and one that you'll look back upon fondly for years to come. Here are some tips to help you recover quicker.

• Keep yourself hydrated during and after your runs. Drink a glass or two of fluids in the half hour after your workout. Keep hydrating until your urine is light yellow or clear.

• Refuel as soon as possible after your runs—and particularly after long or strenuous runs. Details on what and when to eat after your runs are found in chapter 9.

• Sleep seven to eight hours each night. This might seem impossible, but make sleeping a priority and shoot for this target by cutting unnecessary activities, such as watching TV or browsing the Internet.

• Nap! Naps help accelerate the recovery process. While most of us can't fit in a nap during the week, what's stopping you from taking a 90-minute siesta following your long run?

• Wear compression clothing after strenuous runs. Admittedly, the research surrounding the athletic recovery effects of compression clothing isn't airtight, but there's enough evidence to make compression tights and/or calf sleeves worth a try.

• Elite runners have long taken post-workout waist-deep (or nearly so) ice baths of around 10 minutes in water that's 50 to 60 degrees Fahrenheit. Recent research on ice baths and recovery has shown mixed results. That said, my own personal experience as well as that of many ultrarunners I know will still have me jumping in a cold stream after my summer long runs. I recommend wearing socks at least over your toes during an ice bath, as that seems to take the edge off. Also, if you've never before taken an ice bath, fight through the first two minutes. Your acute discomfort decreases soon thereafter.

Runners enjoy a recovery soak after a stage of the GORE-TEX® TransRockies Run. (Photo by author)

Tapering

If you've raced much, chances are you're familiar with the concept of a taper. A taper is a recovery period when overall training volume is reduced in preparation for a focus race. That taper ranges from a few days for a short race to a few weeks for a marathon. As with a marathon, taper for at least two weeks before an ultra and optimally for three weeks. During your taper, maintain the pace of all your training runs, including that of any speed work you might doing. Instead, modify your training by sequentially cutting back on training volume week-to-week by first reducing the length of your long run, longer weekday runs, and any speed work. For instance, in week 1 of a three-week taper you might run 70 percent of your peak weekly mileage before stepping down to 50 percent of your peak mileage the following week. The final week of your taper should be limited to a few shake-out runs of 2 to 5 miles on easy terrain. If you're not antsy and itching to run by the last week of your taper, then you're not tapering enough.

It's great to get one or more key long runs in three weekends before race day. After that, avoid any marathon or longer runs during the final two weekends of your taper. While ultra training often calls for long runs on steep or technical terrain, avoid thoroughly trashing yourself in the two weeks before race day. In general, err on the side of tapering too much rather than not enough. Believe in your training!

Ultra Cross Training

Adam W. Chase

Ultrarunners, regardless of their surface of choice, are often of the belief that "more is better," even if the *more* is a discipline other than running. When you want to condition your body to go and go and go, cross training can be your ultimate savior. One of my favorite practices is to run for two or three hours and immediately jump on my bike or bike trainer and keep the engine running for another hour-plus but without the pounding of continued running. This trains your body's internal systems for the distance without taxing your external systems.

The skills and strengths gained from cross training easily translate to ultrarunning. Hopefully this contribution will make you a better ultrarunner; whether by the strong core you get from circuit training, the limbering and strengthening of muscles from rock climbing, the increased lung capacity gained from Nordic skiing, the high-altitude endurance from mountaineering, the descending skills of mountain biking or mogul skiing, the leg strength gained from snowshoeing, or the muscular balance gained from swimming.

Cross training offers perspective to counter ultrarunning obsessiveness. Cross training can be used as active recovery, allowing you to feel good about not running while pursuing another discipline or developing new skills that enhance your running. By becoming passionate about other athletic endeavors, ultrarunners are more likely to take adequate time away from running when a recovery period is necessary to recuperate from an overuse injury or simply avoid overuse. Knowing that there are alternatives to running certainly helps during a time of injury, boredom, or burnout. Cross training serves as a fine balance that prevents things from getting too far out of whack, both physically and mentally.

Cross training is easily integrated into an ultrarunning routine by substituting a different discipline for a running session or two each week. Execute these cross-training sessions at an equivalent intensity to their running counterparts, as measured by heart rate, effort, and time. For example, after a long trail run on Sunday, replace Monday's recovery run of 45 minutes with a 45-minute swim, bike, or Nordic ski session of equivalent effort.

Only when you exchange a substantial percentage of running workouts for cross training will the cross training detract from your ultrarunning performance. If the primary goal is to be a better ultrarunner, then it's probably important that a majority of your workouts be running. The doctrine of "specificity of training" is an almost obvious principle: The best way to improve at an activity is to train by doing that activity. Ultrarunners should heed the specificity doctrine, but not to the point of ruling out beneficial cross-training workouts.

Depending on your ultrarunning goals, cross training should complement running, but not supplant it. Although cross training is an excellent way of maintaining fitness while giving running muscles some time off, think of it as active recovery in that it should not be so strenuous or depleting that you are left too exhausted to run. Always exercise some caution when trying a new sport—it's easy to strain muscles that are not trained for that specific activity. It is rather disappointing to spoil your running training because of an injury resulting from a cross-training mishap.

The balanced ultrarunner is a rarity, but cross training helps achieve a flexibility that allows you to consider "playing" with other disciplines and work in non-running efforts that serve to include other people in your training. Through such active recovery pursuits, you can involve friends, family, and co-workers, and integrate activities into your travel and social life, without being a single-minded, single-purpose, introverted ultrageek. Hopefully, that flexibility spreads so that you can avoid pushing too hard at your cross training. And keep in mind that every runner is an individual who responds to different types of training. What works for one ultrarunner might be a huge mistake for another. Be sensitive to all your needs plus those of your family, friends, and co-workers.

A holistic approach to ultrarunning keeps your training and racing in perspective. Yes, you need to respect the importance of adequate training, but do not forget the forest for the trees. In addition to proper form, fitness, strength, nutrition, and gear, you will become a better runner if you are balanced and happy with your family, work, and social life. Avoiding overtraining or chronic fatigue and approaching each run with fervor keeps you motivated and assures quality training. You will also run more easily if you're not burdened by stress or lack of recovery, rest, and relaxation. Keep it fun and mix it up whenever possible.

Adam W. Chase is an ultrarunner, adventure racer, snowshoer, Nordic and alpine skier, cyclist, and all around extremely fit guy. He's also the trail editor for Running Times *magazine, president of the American Trail Running Association, trail running community manager for Salomon, and the captain and manager of the Atlas Snow-Shoe Racing Team . . . when he's not out running or cross training.*

Burnout and Fear of Missing Out

What if, for whatever reason, you fail to provide yourself with adequate recovery? You might end up overtrained—aka burned out. Recognizing burnout and taking steps to minimize it are important enough to look at it separately from recovery. In fact, think of recovery as a necessary, preplanned anticipatory of training while recognizing burnout is its reactionary counterpart.

If you are going through a training period and start to feel worn out for more than a couple of days in a row, you may be overtraining. Take it easy for a week. That might involve slashing your weekly mileage by 30 to 40 percent while cutting out your long run. Alternatively, it might involve taking a chunk of days off completely. You are the judge. A good touchstone is to only run when you want and to reengage your training only when you desire to do so rather than when you feel compelled to do so. You might even want to lay low for an additional day or two before fully jumping back into your training regime.

Even during peak training, substituting an emergency break from training can benefit you on race day. In addition to giving your body a chance to recover, you're also giving yourself a mental break. Never underestimate your enthusiasm for running as a key to getting you through your training and successfully to the finish line.

Fear of Missing Out (FOMO) is a frequent cause of fatigue and burnout in the ultrarunning community. As you become aware that you're capable of running vast distances, especially through gorgeous locales or with new and interesting running companions, you may continually add outings and events to indulge your physiological, spiritual, and social desires. While such desires are wonderful motivators, FOMO can leave you taking on additional events without consideration of training benefit or adequate consideration of physiological cost.

If you find yourself unable to decline invitations for a group run, you might have FOMO. If you're unable to resist signing up for every race, you might have FOMO. If you miss a holiday meal to run, you might have FOMO. Beware of FOMO.

Overreaching and Overtraining

To be sure, you stress your body to improve your running. More accurately, it is stress *and* recovery from stress that make you better. To reach your fullest potential you may need to push yourself to the verge of overreaching, which is simply doing too much in the short term. An extended period of stress–recovery imbalance or an extreme imbalance may lead to overtraining. The primary differentiator between overreaching and overtraining is the amount of time it takes to recover. Otherwise, the signs of and recourse for the two states are similar.

The first signs you may notice are persistent fatigue and, perhaps, heavy legs despite a few recovery days. You may want to sleep more than normal, but, at the same time, have difficulty falling or staying asleep. Some athletes also experience weight loss, drop-off in athletic performance, and uncommon thirst.

Your training may take a more consistent hit. For instance, it's a red flag if "you're ramping up training effort, but your results are worse," notes Jeffrey Rocco, an orthopedic surgeon with an interest in sports medicine.

Symptoms can also be psychological. If you experience more anxiety or depression than is typical for you, consider whether you need to change your routine. Likewise, do the same if you experience inappropriate fears or anxiety about your running performance. According to Dr. Rocco, another classic sign is having a hard time putting on your running shoes and getting out the door when that's normally easy.

There are two classic physiological signs that you can prophylactically monitor or use to confirm a hypothesis that you are overreaching or overtraining. First, check to see whether your heart rate is elevated before getting out of bed in the morning. A heart rate that is elevated by at least 10 percent for three or more consecutive mornings suggests that you are at least overreaching. Second, if you wear a heart-rate monitor, a higher heart rate for a given pace is another sign of pushing too far.

In the end, the best diagnosis is having a coach or experienced runner look at your training and lifestyle.

Rest and Recovery

If you find yourself overreaching or overtraining, William Henderson, a physician and exercise physiologist, suggests, "There are two broad areas to think about. If overreaching and overtraining are a mismatch of stress and recovery, then you must fix the balance by both decreasing stress and increasing recovery."

To recover, initially assume that you are overreaching. However, don't completely stop training. Instead, reduce your training volume by 30 to 40 percent. Dr. Henderson notes, "You can keep the intensity in your training. It's all about reducing volume."

If two weeks' recovery doesn't have you feeling better, then more rest is likely warranted. You are overtrained. Continue to modify your training as you did during the first two weeks of rest. Full recovery from overtraining can take months or even years in extreme cases.

Also, examine other aspects of your life. Diet and sleep are crucial for recovery; many of us, however, skimp here. Aim for at least eight hours of sleep. To meet your caloric and nutritional needs, eat enough fat and protein, emphasize whole foods over processed foods, and hydrate well during and after workouts.

Don't stop there, though. Work life, troubled relationships, and other life-related stressors can hold back your training. No matter how difficult, address big issues, too.

The Finish Line

Most endurance athletes who have seriously trained for a few years have experienced one of the fatigue states described here. But the conditions are "as common or more common in amateur athletes as in professional athletes," says Dr. Henderson. "They don't have the ability to focus on stress or especially on recovery that professional athletes do."

The good news is that 90 percent of runners who think they are overtraining are only overreaching. Therefore, most of the time a runner who feels burnout can be back training at full volume in half a month if he or she reducing stressors and increases recovery during that time.

This essay is adapted from the article "The Dreaded FOMO: Manage Stress and Recovery to Maximize Performance" that I wrote for the January 2011 issue of Trail Runner *magazine.*

Do You Need a Coach?

Perhaps it's odd for a training guidebook to consider whether or not you need a coach. No matter, for it's possible for you to use this book as well as a coach to prepare for an ultramarathon. So why in the world would you want to work with a coach anyway? While individual coaching is not for everyone, there are many good reasons why a coach might be right for you.

First, even with available instruction through a guide such as this, many aspiring ultrarunners or ones looking for improvement seek reassurance that they are making the right decisions along the way. Think of it as a mentoring relationship. Such relationships are particularly valuable for a runner who hasn't engaged the local ultrarunning community, as the coach and runner can discuss strategy and logistics in addition to developing a training program.

Such aid might be particularly valuable if your first attempt (or attempts) at ultramarathoning turned out very poorly. Here, a coach reassures you that you can run an ultra well and are on a path to do so.

A coach might also be right if you desire accountability in your training. While a coach in this sort of relationship develops a training program and mentors the runner, simply being there as "Big Brother" is key. Many runners use a coach as a motivating tool to get out there for runs when they otherwise wouldn't. However, some astute runners bring on a coach to make certain they aren't training too much. As is alluded to above, it is quite common for endurance runners and especially those new to ultrarunning to overindulge. Coaches can keep runners accountable regarding weight loss, physical therapy, and other complementary goals.

Even someone who has been running for a long while or has ultramarathon experience can benefit from a coach. Ultramarathon coach Paul DeWitt suggests that coaching may interest "a good runner who is already putting in plenty of effort and getting good results, but has never had a structured training program (that is, he or she never ran in high school or college) and feels like he or she isn't getting the most out of his or her efforts."

Keep in mind that choosing a coach is a personal decision. A coach who is a great fit for one runner isn't necessarily the best for another. Likewise, being a great runner also doesn't guarantee that a person is a great coach, although it certainly doesn't preclude it. Do your homework and pick a coach who fits your needs, desires, and personality. On the last point, if you're not comfortable working with a particular coach, then you're not going to get the most out of that relationship.

If you decide to train with a coach, take a look at the compilation of ultramarathon coaches located at www.iRunFar.com/2008/11/ultramarathon-coaches.html. You can also access the link at www.iRunFar.com/rfp/resources.

Please oblige this one word of caution before moving on. If, after reading this book, you do work with a coach, please fully buy into and adhere to the coach's system. Just as there are multiple ways to skin a cat, there are also multiple ways to prepare for an ultramarathon. Rather than using this book to challenge your coach, think of it as a way to become familiar with words and concepts, as a resource that will allow you to more fully engage with your coach. On the other hand, do not take training or racing methods from this book and intermingle them with your coach's plan for you without first discussing them.

Conclusion

Like all successful running, the crux of ultramarathon training is balancing training volume, intensity, and recovery. In your training, balance long runs with days off and overall training volume with the need for rest periods. Back-to-back long runs and speed work further enhance training, but again call for self-monitoring and prudent recovery. To consistently overstep your body's limits in training serves only to ensure suboptimal performance. With these words of caution in mind, you are now ready to move on to the specific training plans found in chapters 5 and 6.

3

TRAINING FOR COURSE SPECIFICS

In comparison with ultramarathons, most non-ultra road races are very similar, so races of similar length can be run on relatively undifferentiated training. Not so with ultramarathons. Footing, climbs, and descents vary widely. Note that environmental conditions, such as temperature and altitude, can also differ greatly; these are addressed in chapter 13.

Before you sign up for an ultra, investigate what the course conditions are likely to be. If this will be your first ultra, try to match your existing strengths with the course. Perhaps more important, consider whether the course's greatest challenges coincide with your biggest weaknesses. If so, consider choosing a different race for your ultra debut.

After you've chosen your focus race, reflect upon which aspects of the course differ the most from your previous race experience and recent training regimen. Once you identify these aspects, determine how you will prepare for them. Below are guides to help you prepare for difficult footing, pounding pavement, strenuous climbs, and devastating descents.

On Footing

It goes without saying, but attempt to run surfaces similar to those found on the racecourse prior to race day. If the race will be run primarily on dirt trails, it's wise to spend a material portion of your training on trails. Likewise, if you're a steadfast trail runner who is tackling a road ultra, bite the bullet and spend some time hitting the road. Such runs help you prepare both physically and psychologically.

Trails

For the unfamiliar, there's a learning curve when it comes to running trails. From figuring out how far down the trail to look to picking lines through obstacles, you need time on trails to feel comfortable and run well on them. Fortunately, you can make great gains in both technique and mental approach in a short period of time. That said, incremental gains can be made for years to come.

Trail experience is great. However, if you are completely new to trail running, be careful when transiting to conditions where your footing and gait differ significantly from road running. Navigating rocks and roots, maintaining forward momentum on loose surfaces, or landing on an off-camber trail all work your legs differently than roads. You needn't increase the length of your challenging trail runs as slowly as your overall mileage, but do pay attention to how your legs feel a day or two after runs on new terrain. Feel free to bump up the mileage by a few miles in the next outing if you feel good. On the other hand, if you feel lingering soreness in support muscles, don't increase the distance the next time out on that terrain. One of the purposes of trail-specific training is strengthening your support muscles, but don't overdo it in the short term. You can be more aggressive in transitioning from roads to hard-packed dirt trails that lack significant obstacles.

Refining technique and building confidence become increasingly important as a course's footing diverges from the evenness of pavement or benign trail. For example, rocky terrain can bring a talented but conditionally unfamiliar runner to a crawl. Likewise, you greatly benefit from even a small amount of experience when tackling a section of loose, sandy trails during a race.

Once you gain confidence, a boulder field becomes your playground.
(Photo by author)

If possible, it's also a good idea to put in a few training runs with footing conditions that may or may not be present on race day. Uncertain conditions are most often weather-related, such as snow or mud. Don't spend a great deal of time training for "ifs"; just prepare yourself so race day isn't the first time you've ever had to deal with a particular condition.

Look for more specific guidance on trail running in chapter 7.

Roads

Although it might seem silly, it's just as important to prepare specifically for a road ultra. It's true that those with recent road marathon experience are unlikely to have issues with the pavement or the amount of actual running in a 50k road event. However, a trail junkie who rarely hits the road or anyone running a road race of 50 miles or longer serves him- or herself well by running at least a few long training runs on the roads. Even a trail ultra with significant flat portions warrants shifting a number of long runs from the trails to the roads or other flat terrain. Do not underestimate how hard it becomes to run after many miles of flat terrain. Even if you are prepared, you may find yourself secretly wishing for a hill to appear on the horizon.

Tips for Running a Road Ultra

Michael Wardian

Research the Course

Do your homework and know the answer to the following questions before race day:

• Is the race run point-to-point, out-and-back, or on multiple loops?

• Is the course hilly, and, if so, where in the race do the hills fall?

• Historically, what is the weather like during the race?

• What is the current race day forecast?

• Does the course have a windy section, and, if so, where?

The nice thing about road courses is that, once established, they are pretty standard and can be reviewed.

Research Pacers and Support Crews*

If you are interested in having one or more personal pacers run with you on the course, research if, when, and where they are allowed. Be sure to find out what pacers are permit-

---

* Pacers and support crews are fully explained in the "Pre-Race Preparations" section in chapter 12.

ted to and prohibited from doing at that particular race.

If you're interested in having a personal support crew, research whether they are permitted, and, if so, when, where, and in what ways they can assist you. Discuss how you want your crew to help you at each aid station. On race day call out to them in advance if you're modifying your preset assistance at a particular aid station. One advantage of most road ultras is that you'll be able to spot your crew well ahead of time, which isn't always the case in trail ultras.

Research Race Assistance Generally

Research the rules that apply generally to the giving or accepting food and beverages on the course.

- Are you allowed to share with others on the course?
- Can you accept aid outside an aid station?
- If yes, how far outside?
- Do you need to carry water or at least a water receptacle in the case of a cupless race?
- Can the people giving you aid be moving or must they be standing still?
- Take note of any other rules that could result in your disqualification, such as whether your crew can tell you the position of the other athletes.

Research Aid Station Locations and Fare

Look into where aid stations are located on the course and what food and drink those stations will have, so you can plan appropriately. Knowing where you can count on aid, whether supplied by the race or a support crew, should allow you to carry less than a typical trail ultra. For instance, you might not need to carry any fluids and might carry fewer PowerBar Gels. Given that changes in pace are rarely as abrupt in road ultras as in trail ultras, you don't need to carry as many emergency rations.

Note: Please put your trash in a waste receptacle, if possible, or at least drop it at an aid station. Being on the roads is no excuse to litter!

Run the Tangents

Many athletes run farther than necessary. Periodically, look ahead to the next turn in the course and take the straightest line to the inside of that turn. Do, however, to be sure to follow any pre-race instructions and on-course marking with regard to where on the road you must run.

Set Goals

Break your race into sections and set a few goals for each section. These goals can help you keep moving if things don't go as planned.

Prepare for the Monotony

Know that mental and physical breaks come infrequently during a road ultra. Road running is tough. Your legs are continually pounded and the pace is relatively quick. Just as you need to concentrate on your footing during a trail ultra, you need to focus your mind on maintaining your effort during a road ultra.

Be Alert for Traffic and Obstacles

Road ultras often do a good job of protecting participants from cars. Obviously, stay alert if the course or parts of it are open to vehicular traffic. When a road ultra is run on bike paths, the paths often remain open to the public. If that's the case, be alert for walkers, cyclists, dogs, and other moving obstacles. Check to see if the race prohibits headphones for your safety and the safety of others.

Even though obstacles are much less frequent in road ultras, be mindful that you don't step in a pothole, trip on a curb, or run into a sign.

Run Fast and Have Fun

Road ultras are a great place to run a personal best. They can also be a nice way to see a city, town, or park.

Michael Wardian is a husband, father, international shipbroker, and professional runner based in Arlington, Virginia. The USA Track and Field Association (USATF) named him Ultrarunner of the Year for three straight years ('08–'10), during which time he won a combined six USATF road and trail national championships ranging from 50k to 100k.

On Climbing

Many ultras take place in hilly or mountainous terrain. If your next ultra is such a race, be prepared to make it up the next hill or mountain. The good news is that unless you are a front-runner, you'll be walking most grades steeper than a gentle incline. Because of this, hill training for an ultra is much different from hill training for either short trail races or undulating sub-ultra road races. There is nothing wrong with continuing with shorter, more intense hill sessions, but you should consider them speed work rather than ultra climbing practice.

Before diving into hill training, talk to veterans of your focus race to determine the mix of uphill grades on the course. Are all the climbs steep enough to require straight hiking? Are there miles and miles of shallow grades suited to running? Is it a mix?

Once you know what the course is like, tailor your hill training to it. If the course includes many shallow, prospectively runnable inclines, be sure to target some long runs on similar terrain. Do not run these grades with intensity in practice. Run up the grades with the effort of an easy long run. Your goal is to become comfortable running your race day effort on these climbs. As your fitness increases, so might your pace, but the change will happen gradually enough that you needn't worry about running faster in early sessions. Always remember: "Just relax."

A more mountainous course will likely require you to hike many of the climbs. Unless hiking is another of your hobbies, practice hiking before race day. If you enjoy concerted training efforts, by all means go out and repeatedly hike up a long climb. Do not overexert yourself. Concentrate on developing a strong, consistent rhythm that you can maintain up the whole climb and throughout the workout. If you can't stomach the thought of repeatedly walking up the same hill or mountain, include hiking in your long runs by practicing walking on climbs you might otherwise run.

A course like the Western States 100 requires walking climbs
early in the race. (Photo by Glenn Tachiyama)

On Descending

One of the most overlooked aspects of ultramarathon training is descending. There are two reasons for training for downhills: One is to run them faster, and the other is to allow you to finish. Regarding going faster, many new trail runners either flail about when coming down a hill or are overly tentative. Both of these approaches to downhill running are inefficient. For a trail ultra, practice running down some relatively steep hills to help refine your form and give yourself more confidence on the descent. If you often run hilly trails, there's no need to design special runs for this; just be aware of the downhills in your training.

On the other hand, if your race has many thousands of feet of descent, training for downhills can seriously improve your chances of finishing or finishing well. Dead quadriceps muscles can reduce you to a walk, which is particularly frustrating as their most acute failure occurs on descents. When running downhill, your quad muscles work differently than during flat or uphill running. They lengthen as they contract in what is known as an eccentric contraction. You must specifically train your muscles to perform these eccentric contractions, and the best way to do so by running downhill.

As impact forces increase dramatically while descending, it is highly recommended that you find a non-paved surface on which to practice your descents. As a bonus, slightly technical terrain will make your downhill training even more effective. On non-technical terrain you can run smoothly down with minimal braking, thus minimizing the eccentric contraction. Technical terrain forces you to brake, shift weight, and alter your stride length, all of which will enhance the eccentric contractions. In addition, if your race will have technical downhills, it's just good practice to include these in your training.

You won't need to practice descending every week through your training. For those who regularly run hilly trails, training might consist of three or four focused sessions in the two months before the race. The first session might include up to 30 minutes of combined descent time with workouts eventually reaching up to an hour of combined descent time. The longer the downhill, the better, because as you fatigue, you work your muscles differently. Still, you can get an effective workout by running down a short, steep hill ad nauseam.

If you live in a pancake-flat location, you can still prepare your legs for the rigors of a mountain ultra. Stairs are one good substitute for hills. Although you won't be able to practice running smoothly downhill, running down a few flights of stairs will beat up your quads plenty. In fact, the forced stuttering of stair running enhances the training effect just as technical trails do. Lifting is another downhill training tool of the flatland ultrarunner. The most effective methods are leg extensions in which you emphasize slowly lowering the weight back down and, similarly, emphasizing the lowering phase of squats.

Downhill Running in Ultras

Dave Mackey

You peer off the edge of the cliff where your singletrack trail merges onto a 60-degree scree slope below. You tighten your bottle holder onto your skinny waist and launch onto the narrow trail . . . seven-minute, six-minute, five-minute miles click off during the 1,000-meter descent. You feel like a French parapenter in Chamonix . . . *"Whee . . . c'est la vieeeeeee!"*

And then you wake up. Oh yeah . . . you're an ultrarunner.

Now that you're back to reality, know that running downhill in ultras is a lot like running downhill in shorter races, but the extra distance makes for some critical differences. You may desire to fly the descents like Pierre, but to do so will mean that at mile 50 you'll feel more like Pepe. Rein it in a notch, or a couple of notches, in the first half of your long adventure so you don't trash the ol' pegs. Like all pacing in ultras, if you feel you're going too fast, you are.

When it comes to running downhill, you could say you either have it or you don't. However, there are many tricks runners use to better their descents, whether you are a natural downhill rocket or a descending newbie. Darcy Africa, fourth overall at the Hardrock 100 in 2010, says, "Depending on the course I am training for, I may actually focus my training around my downhill running." This certainly worked for Darcy, as she did multiple laps of her local "hill," Mount Sanitas in Boulder, Colorado, to tune her skills for Hardrock success.

Other tricks, such as anticipation of terrain, apply generally to all downhill running, including to ultras. On technical terrain, look about 10 to 15 feet ahead of you, which equates to three to six strides. Like the engineer at the cocktail party trying to get a date, staring at your feet will mean social or, in this case, running collapse. When looking straight downward, you can't anticipate the trail ahead and won't be able to react to an upcoming rock or root. But on non-technical terrain, such as running down a well-groomed dirt road, you can get away with gazing 20 or more feet ahead and focus on increased forward propulsion, putting more effort into forward momentum. A smooth downhill also helps you relax your brain as running one takes less concentration than cranking the rocky stuff.

Run with short strides. This will enable better landing and cushioning on bent rather than outstretched legs. Unless you are trying to overstep a small rocky or rooty patch, overstriding accentuates forces, leading to more fatigued muscles and pounded leg joints.

Ultrarunner and Hardrock veteran Scott Jaime is a big NASCAR fan who continually repeats his mantra, "Keep the shiny side up," when racing ultras. Now I, too, repeat, "Keep the shiny side up, keep the shiny side up, keep the shiny side up," to myself as I descend technical terrain. This mantra keeps me focused on the following: leaning forward, picking foot placement two or three steps in advance, lifting my feet by driving my knees, and keeping my elbows nice and wide for balance.

In longer mountain races, take in the electrolytes on a regular basis. One of the first things to go when electrolytes are low is fine-motor movement and coordination. For example, I know I'm low when I start to skim the top of obstacles.

Scott also finds that when his fueling suffers in ultras, so does his downhill running. "It's good practice to routinely get in the fluids that will ultimately determine the fate of the race. They can also help prevent taking a nasty spill on a technical descent."

Stay balanced. Keep your shoulders perpendicular to the trail and your center of gravity just in front of your hips. Try to keep your arms out slightly and bent so as to make micro-adjustments in balance on the fly, acting like an animal's tail in midflight. In ultras you may feel sore in your upper arms and shoulders after a long hilly race or training run. This is typical, but the more you train and race, the stronger you become. Consider incorporating some upper-extremity strengthening, as well as core work, to be better balanced and strong in the later miles.

Most of all, have fun out there! If you are a beginner ultra runner or new to trails, then downhill running can be a real hoot as your abilities develop.

Dave Mackey has won numerous USATF national titles and twice earned USATF Ultrarunner of the Year honors. Mackey holds the course records at the Miwok 100k and Bandera 100k as well as the fastest known time* for a Grand Canyon double crossing.

* See the afterword for more on fastest known times.

4

USING THE TRAINING PLANS

Chapters 5 and 6 outline six training plans, with each outlining a 24-week day-by-day plan. Before jumping into these plans, it's important to know how to use them. Read on to determine if you have a sufficient training base to start preparing for an ultra or how to develop one if you don't. Next, become familiar with how the training plans deal with training mileage and time, how you should add specificity to your training, how to incorporate speed work into the training plans (if you choose to do so), and how to properly approach rest. Then, examine the myriad ways to modify the training plans for your individual needs. Finally, learn the roles preparatory races, consistency, and self-coaching have in your ultra training.

Both this chapter and the two that follow rely heavily on chapters 2 and 3. If you have not read them, please do so prior to beginning any of the training plans in this book.

Presumption of Training Background

The training plans found in this book presume that you've run a marathon in the past year or have trained at 35 to 40 miles per week for at least four of the past six months. If you fall short of these criteria, please be patient and build a training base before embarking on your ultramarathon journey. Either gradually build your weekly mileage until you can comfortably run 35 to 40 miles per week for a few weeks, or follow a novice marathon training program in full regardless of whether or not you run the marathon. It is true that the first few weeks of chapter 5's 50-mile-per-week plans start with mileage in the low-30-mile-per-week range. However, these are easy weeks in which you transition into consistent training. They should not be your longest-ever training weeks.

Time Versus Mileage Versus Trail Mileage

Most runners track their training volume by distance covered, whether that be in miles, kilometers, leagues, or parsecs. That said, a good number of runners base their training entirely on time. Both approaches are valid. Because this book must choose one measure, it will follow majority rules and use distance and, in particular, miles in prescribing overall training volume. The fact that most ultras are of a fixed length and that you should make discrete steps toward that distance also counsels toward logging training in miles.

If, however, you prefer training based on time, by all means continue to do so. Most days, simply translate the prescribed run from miles into minutes based on what you estimate your training pace to have been for an everyday training run in your last training cycle. This estimate should take into account the terrain on which you typically run, be it road or trail, flat or hilly. For long runs, estimate the necessary duration by using the estimated pace you would run if training (not racing) on the focus race course.

Training Specificity

This is a good place to remind you about training specificity. If your focus race is on trails, aim to run at least three or four of the weekly long runs, including one of the two or three very longest training runs in these training plans, primarily on trails. Not only do these runs build trail running skills and musculature, but they also ensure that you spend adequate time on your feet in training. *Time on feet* is a phrase that's commonly thrown out during informal discussions about trail ultramarathon training. The concept behind the phrase is that speed is not of the essence during long training runs. In fact, sometimes it's beneficial to complete a route in more rather than less time.

If your focus ultra is a road ultra or flat, non-technical trail ultra, you can run the prescribed mileage for all of your long runs on the road. That's not to say you should run all of those long runs on the road, just that you don't have to do any mileage conversion.

Speed Work

If you choose to include speed work in your ultra training, be sure to warm up for at least a mile and a half and to cool down for at least a mile after each session. Never skimp on the cool-down just because it will put you slightly over your prescribed mileage for the day.

While the training plans that follow assign daily and weekly training volume in miles, speed work volume is assigned by time. More precisely, the plans assign speed work as total time run at speed, excluding recovery breaks. Assigning the speed work this way gives you maximum flexibility to choose the type of speed work you want to run as well as how to divide it up. However, feel free to design your workouts in terms of distance (6 x 800 meters, for instance, or 4-mile tempo run) if you are able to roughly estimate the time it takes you to cover the set distances. It's not a big deal to slightly overshoot the duration at speed for a given workout due to a miscalculation or the desire of your training partner(s) to run a particular workout. Just don't make it a habit of running more speed work than is prescribed. The purpose of the time limits on speed work is to minimize the risk of overtraining or fatigue-based injury.

Intervals

The speed work durations in the training plans are designed with interval training, as described in chapter 2, in mind. As such, break that time up into true intervals, long hill repeats, or fartleks. For the benefit of example, let's suppose you run 18 to 20 minutes of speed work on a given Thursday.

Some possible interval workouts include:

• 6 to 8 repeats of 800 meters (m) with 400 meters rest.

• A ladder of 400m, 800m, 1200m, 1200m, 800m, 400m with a recovery jog of half the distance of the previous interval. Faster runners might add a 1600m interval in the middle of the ladder.

• 3 x 1 mile with a 3-minute recovery jog.

(Keep in mind that these workouts are only meant to be exam-

Hill workouts build strength and endurance. (Photo by Glenn Tachiyama)

ples; you may run fewer or additional repeats of a given distance in the prescribed time.)

Long hill repeats often call for time-based repeats such as 6 x 3 minutes or 4 x 5 minutes with a recovery jog back down to where you started the repeat. If your hill isn't much longer than a minute when running your workout, determine your average time to the top and do some rough back-of-the-envelope calculations to determine how many repeats to run.

I won't give you any recommendations for breaking up the cumulative time for a fartlek. Go see what you enjoy most. That's the whole point of fartleks!

Tempo Runs

Workouts based on longer "tempo" workouts are described in chapter 2. Tempo workouts and related cruise intervals are straightforward enough that no examples are needed beyond what's found in chapter 2.

If you are an experienced marathoner who chooses to run a tempo workout, consider running 25 to 50 percent more than the prescribed speed work time. Less experienced runners should build their tempo runs to at least 20 minutes. The key word is *build*, as a runner who's never done speed work may want to log tempo runs of 10, 12, and 15 minutes before tackling a full 20 minutes.

No-Speed-Work Option

As mentioned in chapter 2, speed work is unnecessary when training for ultras. For those opting out of speed work, run a more difficult route on Thursday, whether hillier or more technical, than you normally do; or if you stick to your usual terrain, run 2 to 3 miles more than prescribed for the day. The schedule takes into account the added fatigue of speed work with a recovery day on Friday, so you'll still be fine to tackle your long run on the weekend.

Rest

Rest is just that—rest. When training calls for a rest day, either take the day off from exercise or do some light-to-moderate cross training for up to an hour.* Although it may be counterintuitive, a light cross-training day (as opposed to a day with no exercise) is most useful following a particularly demanding training run or ultra. This type of cross training, known as active recovery, is discussed in the "Recovery" section of chapter 2.

Tailor Your Training Plan

Despite the greatest care, it is impossible to create one or two training plans for a given distance that meet everyone's needs perfectly. That's another reason why some runners like to work with coaches. For the rest of us, it's often easy enough to tailor a training plan to suit our needs. This section explains ways to modify any of the training plans in this book.

Days of the Week

We all live our lives on different schedules, and each runner's training fits into that schedule differently. I'm here to tell you that it's easy to move elements of your training schedule around to suit your needs. One common and easy change would be to switch your Saturday and Sunday runs so that your longest run is usually on Sunday. Note, however, that if your schedule calls for back-to-back long runs, try to keep the longer of the two runs on Saturday. Although it's okay if you can't.

As for the rest of the week, it's all right to move your training around so long as you alternate hard and easy days and avoid logging two hard days in a row on a regular basis. For those who move their

---

* If the activity is particularly light, such as a casual bike ride about town, longer duration cross training sessions are fine. Just make sure that they enhance, not detract from your subsequent workouts.

speed work and are looking for more detailed advice, here you go . . . feel free to move it to either Tuesday or Wednesday. When you switch your speed work to Tuesday, reschedule your longest weekday run for Thursday, with Wednesday remaining a recovery run. Although it's less desirable, it would be acceptable to run your speed work on Tuesday, to run your longest weekday run on Wednesday, and then to run the recovery run originally scheduled for Wednesday on Thursday. On the other hand, if you move your speed work to Wednesday, run your longest weekday run on Thursday with Wednesday's recovery run moved to Tuesday. You do not want to run moderately long on Tuesday followed by speed work on Wednesday.

Days Per Week

Runners are creatures of habit. We find what works and we stick with it. This is often true of how many days per week we run. We are four-, five-, six-, or seven-day-a-week runners. Whatever your preference, chances are you can stick with it through any of this book's training plans. In general, four-, five-, or six-day weeks would work best for the 50-mile-per-week plans, while the 70-mile-per-week plans are better suited for five-, six-, or seven-day-per-week runners. Indeed, many 70-mile-per-week runners will run six or seven days per week.

For the runner who prefers a four-day running week and follows one of the 50-mile-per-week training plans, there are two options, both of which call for taking Wednesdays off. For those who want to stick to the target mileage, add 3 miles to each Tuesday and 2 miles to each Thursday. For those on a 70-mile-per-week training plan, it would be difficult to remain injury-free running only four days per week.

Any training plan in the book is suitable for a six-day-per-week approach. To make it happen, simply scavenge a few miles from both your Wednesday and Sunday runs. It's preferable to log those miles on Friday rather than Monday so you can have a break after your higher-mileage weekend. However, I highly recommend sticking with a five-day week for weeks with back-to-back longer runs. For those following a 50-mile-per-week training plan, this includes Sundays on which you run 10 miles or more.

Seven-day running weeks are best saved for those ramping up to 70 miles per week during peak training. Be aware running a 70-mile week in ultra training differs significantly from a 70-mile week in marathon training. The longer and more numerous long runs, back-to-backs, and more time on feet counsels toward running the mileage in six days with a rest day. If a seven-day week is for you, I'd recommend modifying your training schedule per the six-day week suggestions in the preceding paragraph and then adding an additional 4 to 6 miles per week in the form of a Monday run.

There's no need for someone following a 50-mile-per-week plan to run seven days each week. In fact, I highly recommend taking at least one day off every week, preferably Friday, as noted above.

Altering Weekly Mileage

Each of the training plans in this book is built around one of two peak training week mileage totals—50 or 70 miles per week. However, it's possible to modify these training plans to provide for other desired peak weekly mileages so long as you follow a couple of key principles.

First, respect the long runs, as they are the basis of your ultra training. Don't routinely cut them short or lengthen them. Similarly, leave any back-to-back long runs unaltered with the exception of very high-mileage runners, who may add a few miles to the shorter of the runs.

Second, add or subtract miles from your weekly totals relatively evenly throughout the training plan. For instance, it's ill advised to run the prescribed mileage for week 1 though week 12 before suddenly adding an extra 10 or 15 miles to every week.

Third, aim to alternate harder and easier days on weekdays. Don't simply add miles to your easy days until they resemble your hard days or subtract from your longer weekday runs until they look like your easy days. Training is based around stressing your body before letting it recover.

Finally, you should have significant experience if you intend to run 80 or more miles per week! Use your ingenuity and presumed training experience to log the extra miles, whether it's by adding more miles to individual runs, running seven days per week, and/or running twice some days. It's okay to log high mileage, but don't overdo it. The easiest way to ruin ultramarathon performance is by overtraining.

It is possible to run a 50k or 50-mile on fewer than 50 miles per week. How to do so is explained in chapter 5.

Jumping into the Deep End: Starting Training Plans at Week 5

Experienced marathoners who have consistently trained at 50 miles per week or more, excluding recovery weeks and rest periods, over the past year may begin with week 5 in the provided training schedules. However, a few things need to align for that jump to make sense. Here are two scenarios in which I have no reservations with you proceeding directly to week 5. In one scenario, you ran a marathon (or a training run of similar length) four or so weeks before starting your ultra training. In the interim, you've taken time to recover, but have gradually returned to running regularly and comfortably logs two-thirds of your normal training volume by the week prior to starting the ultra training program. Alternatively, you're already running maintenance mileage within 20 percent of your peak mileage with long runs of at least 16 miles every few weeks.

Preparatory Races

Unless you live in a hotbed of ultrarunning, you're unlikely to find tune-up races that fit exactly into your training plan. Fortunately, there's no need for that fit to be perfect. Tune-up races can usually be moved two or three weeks in either direction with little effect. In fact, you could run a prescribed tune-up race up to a month early, if absolutely necessary.

There are a couple of things to keep in mind when moving tune-up races around. First, move both the week prior to and following the race. Moving the entire week of the race ensures that you rest before the race, while moving the entire week after the race ensures adequate recovery. Second, avoid scheduling tune-up races closer than three weeks apart, and do not schedule them on back-to-back weekends. Finally, avoid running any tune-up races within three weeks of your focus ultra.

The training schedules include a recovery week after each preparatory race;* however, your body will react differently to each race. While you're quite likely to experience muscle soreness for a few days after these races, if toward the end of the week following each such race you continue to have low energy or you struggle through your runs, please heed the advice in chapter 2 regarding rest, recovery, and overtraining. It's far better to fully recover than to run yourself into the ground.

Consistency Is Critical

Ultramarathon success is built on consistent training. While we must remain flexible in adapting to injuries, illness, and life, it's important to train consistently over the course of a season. Don't let small setbacks throw off your training rhythm. Aim for relentless forward progress in training. The benefits of training consistency

---

* The 50k training plans do not prescribe a preparatory race; however, each gives the option of running a scheduled 26 mile training run in a marathon.

only increase when carried on into multiple training seasons.

I do not encourage long-term running streaks, as I feel there are times when it's best to take a break from running. That said, building up a streak, whether every day or every day on which a workout is prescribed, is a great way to build momentum early in a training cycle.

Coach Yourself

As mentioned earlier in this chapter, it's impossible to create a training plan that works for everyone, hence all the modification options. While the training plans provide guidance, you must carefully consider your own running background, life circumstances, and goal race when using the following training plans. This book provides you with the tools to be your own ultramarathon coach, so please do modify the plans to best meet your needs.

5

TRAINING FOR 50K, 50-MILE, AND 100K RACES

So you want to run an ultra after all. Well, it's time to get training! If you're looking to train for races between 50k (31 miles) and 100k (62) miles, this chapter provides the training instructions for doing so. There are four day-by-day training plans with two for the 50k and two for races of 40 miles to 100k. Each pair of training plans has an option for runners seeking to peak at 50 or 70 miles per week. And don't worry, you can run a 50-mile or shorter ultramarathon on less than 50 miles per week of training. This chapter contains directions for doing that, too.

As you read these training plans, please refer back to the "Speed Work" and "Tailor Your Training Plans" sections in chapter 4 for general instructions on these specific plans.

Modifications for Running Less than 50 Miles per Week

It's possible to train for a 50k or 50-miler on less than 50 miles per week. Although physically possible, I can't recommend trying either distance on less than 40 miles per week during peak training. If you want to reduce the training volume of one of the 50-mile-per-week training plans in this chapter, cross train rather than run on Wednesday to cut your first 3 to 5 miles each week. After that, shave 1 to 3 miles off your Tuesday and Sunday runs until you reach your desired weekly mileage. Don't regularly trim runs to less than 4 miles.

In theory, a 100k is not that much farther than a 50-miler. However, realize that those additional 12 miles will be run at or slower than the slowest pace of a 50-miler. That translates into a minimum of two hours of additional running, but more likely three or even four more. In order to have a successful go at the 100k distance, please log the full volume of one of these training plans.

Training for a 50k Race

The 50k distance is a perfect step up from marathons to ultras. When run on the roads or flat, benign trails, a 50k is much the same as a marathon. Yes, the pace is tempered from the start and many more calories are consumed, but a 50k on a mild course only takes an hour longer than a marathon, give or take half an hour.

The difference between a road marathon and a trail 50k grows more significant as the terrain becomes hillier and the footing more technical. Not only do more difficult terrain and technical trails require new skills, but they also mean a runner spends significantly more time running a hilly trail ultra than a road marathon. In fact, a 50k on a rugged course can easily take one and a half to as much as two times as long as a road marathon. As suggested in David Horton's essay later in this chapter, do not underestimate the 50k distance.

All that said, training for a 50k is a lot like training for a marathon. In fact, if you've run a marathon in the past few months, chances are you could finish a 50k with a few months of training. Still, a longer period of dedicated ultramarathon training allows you to learn necessary skills, incorporate training specificity, and build confidence before stepping up to 50k. Make sure to include a significant amount of race-specific training described in chapter 3. In all seriousness, this may be the most important aspect of your 50k training. It is crucial to prepare adequately for the terrain and footing found in an ultra. This is particularly true for a road marathoner looking to make an ultra debut at a trail 50k.

Below are 50k training plans for 50 and 70 mile-per-week runners, but, first, I'll provide a 50k-training option if you would prefer to stick with a familiar marathon-training plan.

A 50k, such as the Speedgoat 50k in Utah, can have
over 10,000 feet of climbing! (Photo by author)

Option to Modify a Marathon Training Plan for a 50k Race

While there are two 50k training plans in this chapter, it's also possible to train for a 50k by following your favorite marathon training plan with a few key modifications that probably sound familiar from chapters 2 and 3. Many marathoners have used a particular marathon training plan with success, train with others who follow a marathon training plan, or both. The modifications below allow you to tune those marathon plans to train for a 50k. The remainder of this book provides invaluable advice regarding the multitude of supplementary topics to bring you up to speed on training for, planning for, and racing a 50k. *Relentless Forward Progress* is the reference book that should answer your most pressing questions.

The first modification to a marathon training plan is to limit speed work to once a week and to generally keep speed work intervals to two minutes or longer. If a speed session is removed, replace it with a run that's 2 or 3 miles longer than the next longest weekday run.

Training for a 50k also requires greater emphasis on long runs. For most plans, that means building up long runs faster so that you can log eight or more 18-mile or longer long runs, at least two or three runs in the 22-to-24-mile range, and, if possible, one marathon-distance training run. While the marathon-distance run can be logged in a marathon, it should not be "raced." Along with the physiological benefits, the primary purposes of the marathon-distance training run are to practice fueling and hydration as well as refamiliarizing yourself with running on tired legs.

Quick Reference Guide

The following table indicates where crucial information regarding the training plan can be found.

Subject	Page(s)
Active recovery	47, 52-4
Back-to-back (B2B) long runs	35-6
Long runs	33-4
Modification of training plan—general	80-85
Speed work	37-46
Training for course specifics	61-73, 76-7

Training Plan for a 50k Race on 50 Miles per Week

Week	Mon	Tues	Wed	Thurs	Fri	Sat	Sun	Total	Thurs Speed Work Duration
1	Rest	6	5	6	Rest	12	5	34	No speed work
2	Rest	6	5	6	Rest	14	5	36	No speed work
3	Rest	6	5	6	Rest	14	5	36	No speed work
4	Rest	5	3	5	Rest	12	5	30	No speed work
5	Rest	7	5	7	Rest	14	5	38	12-15 mins
6	Rest	7	5	7	Rest	16	5	40	12-15 mins
7	Rest	7	5	7	Rest	16	5	40	15-18 mins
8	Rest	6	4	6	Rest	14	5	35	12-15 mins
9	Rest	10	5	7	Rest	18	5	45	15-18 mins
10	Rest	10	5	7	Rest	12	10	44	15-18 mins
11	Rest	7	5	7	Rest	20	5	44	No speed work
12	Rest	6	4	6	Rest	14	5	35	18-20 mins
13	Rest	9	5	5	Rest	24	5	48	20-25 mins
14	Rest	7	5	7	Rest	18	10	47	20-25 mins
15	Rest	6	4	6	Rest	14	10	40	20-25 mins
16	Rest	10	5	5	Rest	26	4	50	15-18 mins
17	Rest	7	5	7	Rest	18	12	49	20-25 mins
18	Rest	6	4	6	Rest	14	10	40	20-25 mins
19	Rest	7	5	4	Rest	20	14	50	No speed work
20	Rest*	4	4	6	Rest	14	5	33	10-15 mins
21	Rest	7	5	7	Rest	24	5	48	20-25 mins
22	Rest	7	5	7	Rest	16	Rest	35	18-20 mins
23	Rest	5	Rest	7	Rest	10	5	27	12-15 mins
24	4	Rest	3	Rest	2	**31**	Rest	40	No speed work

Shading indicates a recovery or taper week.
Bold indicates a race.
Note that in week 16 you have the option of running a marathon. If you choose to do so, do not race it all out!
* Active recovery is particularly important on this day!

Training Plan for a 50k Race on 70 Miles per Week

Week	Mon	Tues	Wed	Thurs	Fri	Sat	Sun	Total	Thurs Speed Work Duration
1	Rest	7	5	7	Rest	12	6	37	No speed work
2	Rest	7	5	7	Rest	14	6	39	12-15 mins
3	Rest	8	5	8	Rest	16	6	43	12-15 mins
4	Rest	7	5	7	Rest	14	5	38	No speed work
5	Rest	8	6	8	Rest	18	8	48	15-18 mins
6	Rest	8	6	8	Rest	18	8	48	15-18 mins
7	Rest	10	6	8	Rest	20	8	52	18-20 mins
8	Rest	8	5	7	Rest	14	6	40	12-15 mins
9	Rest	10	6	8	Rest	20	10	54	18-20 mins
10	Rest	12	6	10	Rest	16	14	58	20-25 mins
11	Rest	14	6	8	Rest	24	10	62	18-20 mins
12	Rest	10	6	8	Rest	16	10	50	20-25 mins
13	Rest	14	6	10	Rest	24	12	66	18-20 mins
14	Rest	14	6	10	Rest	20	16	66	No speed work
15	Rest*	6	6	10	Rest	16	10	48	20-25 mins
16	Rest	14	6	10	Rest	26	8	64	20-25 mins
17	Rest	14	6	10	Rest	22	16	68	No speed work
18	Rest*	6	6	12	Rest	16	10	50	20-25 mins
19	Rest	10	8	4	Rest	24	16	46	No speed work
20	Rest*	4	8	10	Rest	16	12	50	20-25 mins
21	Rest	14	8	10	Rest	25	12	69	20-25 mins
22	Rest	10	6	10	Rest	20	5	52	18-20 mins
23	Rest	8	5	8	Rest	10	5	36	15-18 mins
24	5	Rest	4	Rest	2	**31**	Rest	42	No speed work

Shading indicates a recovery or taper week.

Bold indicates a race.

Note that in week 16 you have the option of running a marathon. If you choose to do so, do not race it all out!

* Active recovery is particularly important on this day!

Training for 40-Mile to 100k Races

While it's true that a lightly modified marathon training plan can prepare you for a 50k, the same is not true when training for a 40-mile, 50-mile, or 100-kilometer (62-mile) race. With this move up in race distance, the marathon transforms from a revered racing distance to a training run.

Indeed, plan on running a 50k race in the lead-up one of these longer ultramarathons. This prerequisite ultra is an arena for mental transition as much as physical development. Whereas in a 50k not taking in enough calories or going out too hard might create 5 or 10 miles of suffering, the same mistakes in a 50-mile or 100k race might mean 20 or more highly unpleasant miles. Specifically, there's a tune-up 50k found in week 19 of both plans. Run as a very long training run rather than a focused race effort, the tune-up race allows you to come to peace with the value of easy pacing for very long efforts. In addition, you'll get a chance to dial in your hydration, fueling, and gear, as well as building fitness and confidence.

A small number of very long training runs ranging from 24 to 31 miles also become much more important with moderate-length ultras. These long training runs are proving grounds for your nutrition, hydration, gear, and pacing plans. It's no surprise that they're also important for cardiovascular and muscular system enhancement. In particular, you'll notice which muscles, large or small, are your weakness and have a chance to strengthen them before your big race. You'll also get to experience the metabolic and hormonal changes that occur during ultra-distance endurance efforts.

Training Plan for Races of 40 Miles to 100k on 50 Miles per Week

Week	Mon	Tues	Wed	Thurs	Fri	Sat	Sun	Total	Thurs Speed Work Duration
1	Rest	6	5	6	Rest	12	5	34	No speed work
2	Rest	6	5	6	Rest	14	5	36	No speed work
3	Rest	6	5	6	Rest	16	5	38	No speed work
4	Rest	5	3	5	Rest	14	5	32	No speed work
5	Rest	7	5	7	Rest	16	5	40	12-15 mins
6	Rest	7	5	7	Rest	18	5	42	12-15 mins
7	Rest	7	5	7	Rest	18	5	42	15-18 mins
8	Rest	6	4	6	Rest	14	5	35	12-15 mins
9	Rest	10	5	7	Rest	20	5	47	15-18 mins
10	Rest	10	5	7	Rest	12	10	44	15-18 mins
11	Rest	7	5	7	Rest	22	5	46	No speed work
12	Rest	6	4	6	Rest	14	5	35	18-20 mins
13	Rest	9	5	7	Rest	24	5	50	20-25 mins
14	Rest	7	5	7	Rest	18	10	47	20-25 mins
15	Rest	6	4	6	Rest	14	10	40	20-25 mins
16	Rest	10	5	7	Rest	24	5	51	15-18 mins
17	Rest	7	5	7	Rest	18	10	47	20-25 mins
18	Rest	6	4	6	Rest	14	10	40	20-25 mins
19	Rest	7	5	3	Rest	**31**	Rest*	46	No speed work
20	Rest*	6	4	6	Rest	14	5	35	10-15 mins
21	Rest	7	5	7	Rest	25	5	49	20-25 mins
22	Rest	5	5	7	Rest	18	Rest	35	18-20 mins
23	Rest	5	Rest	7	Rest	10	5	27	12-15 mins
24	4	Rest	3	Rest	2	**50**	Rest	59	No speed work

Shading indicates a recovery or taper week.
Bold indicates a race.
* Active recovery is particularly important on this day!

Training Plan for Races of 40 Miles to 100k on 70 Miles per Week

Week	Mon	Tues	Wed	Thurs	Fri	Sat	Sun	Total	Thurs Speed Work Duration
1	Rest	7	5	7	Rest	12	6	37	No speed work
2	Rest	7	5	7	Rest	14	6	39	12-15 mins
3	Rest	8	5	8	Rest	16	6	43	12-15 mins
4	Rest	7	5	7	Rest	14	5	38	No speed work
5	Rest	8	6	8	Rest	18	8	48	15-18 mins
6	Rest	8	6	8	Rest	18	8	48	15-18 mins
7	Rest	10	6	8	Rest	20	8	52	18-20 mins
8	Rest	8	5	7	Rest	14	6	40	12-15 mins
9	Rest	10	6	8	Rest	20	10	54	18-20 mins
10	Rest	12	6	10	Rest	16	14	58	20-25 mins
11	Rest	14	6	8	Rest	24	10	62	18-20 mins
12	Rest	10	6	8	Rest	16	10	50	20-25 mins
13	Rest	14	6	10	Rest	24	12	66	18-20 mins
14	Rest	14	6	10	Rest	20	18	68	No speed work
15	Rest*	12	6	10	Rest	16	10	54	20-25 mins
16	Rest	12	6	10	Rest	24	12	64	20-25 mins
17	Rest	12	6	10	Rest	22	18	68	No speed work
18	Rest*	10	6	12	Rest	16	10	54	20-25 mins
19	Rest	10	8	4	Rest	31	Rest*	53	No speed work
20	Rest*	6	8	10	Rest	16	12	52	20-25 mins
21	Rest	14	8	10	Rest	25	12	69	20-25 mins
22	Rest	10	6	10	Rest	20	5	52	18-20 mins
23	Rest	8	5	8	Rest	10	5	36	15-18 mins
24	5	Rest	4	Rest	2	50	Rest	61	No speed work

Shading indicates a recovery or taper week.
Bold indicates a race.
* Active recovery is particularly important on this day!

Training for Your First 50 Miler*

Dr. David Horton

A lot of folks think that you should try a 50k before your first 50-miler. I am not sure if I agree with this thought. Too many runners think that a 50k is just 5 miles longer than a marathon and end up running it at or near marathon pace. This can and will likely end in disaster. On the other hand, if you pick a 50-miler as your first ultra, you will definitely go out slower, run slower, and probably have a better first ultramarathon experience.

With this in mind, many people would assume that a normal progression would be running 5ks, 10ks, 10-milers, marathons, and then a 50-miler. I think that is appropriate in most cases. However, I don't think you necessarily have to run a marathon before you run an ultra. For that matter, I know of a couple of runners for whom their first running race was an ultra. That said, most runners still won't attempt an ultra, especially a 50-miler, after having finished a marathon or two. The thought of going almost twice as far, hurting twice as much, and training twice as hard is unbearable.

You don't hurt twice as much. In fact, ultras are easier than marathons. Marathons are much more intense, and most people run the entire distance. In ultras, only the very elite are able to run 50 miles nonstop. Some elite runners (who run all the way) are beaten by other runners who mix in walking with their running.

The longer you've been running, the better your chances are

---

* Much of the advice in this essay is largely applicable to running a first ultra in general.

of finishing your first ultra. I don't know the minimum time that you should have been running before you start training for your first ultra, but I suggest six months or more. After picking out your race, try to allow three months of gradually increasing your mileage to a peak of 40 to 50 miles per week.

The day before your long run should be very easy. Take off the day after your long run.

Do I have to run all the way in my long runs? No. In fact, one problem that many first-time ultrarunners encounter is that they have difficulty with the amount of walking that must be done in their first ultra. They have trained to run but not walk. I suggest that you mix in some walking in your long training runs. Walk up some of the short steep hills or run a specific amount of time and then walk a specific amount of time. In my first several ultras, I ran 25 minutes and walked 5 minutes until I got tired; then I would change to 20 and 5, and later 15 and 5. If you're training on trails or on hilly roads, just walk the uphills and run everything else.

The key principle for any runner is specificity. Your training should mimic as closely as possible the racing terrain and conditions. If you're doing an ultra on trails, then your long run should be on trails. If you are racing at altitude or your race includes long climbs and descents, then you need to prepare for those variables, if possible. Do I have to run on trails every day if I'm going to race on trails? *No.* I usually do only my long run on trails. Occasionally, I will do two training runs on trails in one week. I also think that you should do one moderately long run per week, usually on the road at a good pace (as fast or faster than your normal daily pace). A relatively easy day should follow and precede this day as well.

Your goal in your first ultra should be to finish. Try not to think about any particular time or person you want to beat or keep up with. How long will it take you to finish 50 miles? When I first started running 50-milers, I was told to multiply my marathon time by two and add two hours. Thus a three-and-a-half-hour marathoner should be able to finish a 50-miler in nine hours. I think this is fairly accurate for road 50s but not trail 50s. A better gauge for trail 50s is to multiply your marathon time by three.

Dr. David Horton, a professor of exercise science at Liberty University, may have congratulated more runners upon finishing their first ultramarathon than anyone else during his many years as a race director. As an ultrarunner, Dr. Horton twice won the Hardrock 100 and has established fastest known times on the Appalachian, Pacific Crest, and Long Trails. He also finished third at the 1995 Trans-America race and is one of nine finishers of the notorious Barkley Marathons.

This essay is adapted from the article "The Ultimate Running Experience: Completing Your First Ultra-Marathon" on Dr. Horton's website, www.extremeultrarunning.com.

TRAINING FOR A 100-MILE RACE

If there's a big step up from a marathon to a shorter ultramarathon, then there's one giant leap up to a 100-miler. This leap is 10 percent physical and 90 percent mental. While you need to log the miles in training, it's even more important that you develop the correct mental approaches to running for 20 hours or more. These critical approaches include fueling, hydrating, walking, and problem solving, which are laid out in full throughout this book.

In general, the training for a 100-miler looks much the same as it does for a 50-miler. There's less speed work as well as more frequent and longer long runs than marathon training. There are, however, a few key differences in training for a 100-miler as opposed to a 50-miler. To start, training for a 100-miler requires lengthening a few of your longest long runs. This will include running both a 50k (week 14) and a 50-miler or 100k (week 19) as tune-up races in the months leading up to the 100-miler. The 100-mile training plans also place a bit more emphasis on back-to-backs (B2Bs), even if the shorter of the B2B runs is only moderately long. These changes mean a general shift in training mileage to the weekend.

All of this assumes you are ready to tackle the 100-mile distance. At a minimum, you should meet the presumed level of background spelled out in chapter 4. In brief, this presumed background calls for you to have run a marathon in the past year or to have trained at 35 to 40 miles per week for at least four of the past six months. However, while this is a fine background for starting to train for a 50-miler, it's preferable to have a more substantial training history heading into 100-mile training. Ideally, you already consider your-self an ultramarathoner. I recommend having trained for and run ultramarathons for at least one six-month season before starting to train for 100-miler. Alternatively, a runner who on average runs a marathon more than once every other month could ramp up to the 100-mile distance, although he or she would face a steep learning curve.

While I'm reticent to discourage anyone from striving for their goals, I question the need to either run a 100-miler as your first ultra or to progress through the 50k, 50-mile, and on to the 100-mile during your first season as an ultrarunner. Enthusiasm is priceless. It is also remarkably abundant and self-reinforcing in the ultrarunning world. Why not channel that initial enthusiasm toward building a strong ultrarunning foundation and enjoying your newfound running range? When I jumped into ultrarunning, I followed my first 50k with a 71-mile race just five weeks later. Physically, I could have jumped up to the 100-mile distance in the months that followed, but I chose not to. I knew it would be a supremely rewarding adventure, which it eventually was, but I wanted to enjoy exploring the 50k and 50-mile distances first. More important, I wanted to leave a new challenge to strive for, to experience, and to savor. I ask you, why not let the mystery be? At least for a little while.

This chapter provides two 100-mile training plans, one each for the 50- and 70-mile-per-week runners. Unlike the training plans in the preceding chapter, the peak weekly training mileage in these plans slightly exceeds the labeled mileage amount. By its nature, training for a longer ultra is "lumpier" than 5k, 10k, marathons, and even shorter ultras. Longer long runs, B2Bs, and tune-up ultras on the weekends mean that you'll overshoot the target mileage some weeks even if you hold your weekday runs to a minimum. The training plans compensate for these over-mileage weeks. As a reminder, refer back to the "Speed Work" and "Tailor Your Training Plans" sections in chapter 4 for general instructions on these specific plans.

The 100-mile training plans also work well for 24-hour and 135-mile races. However, these races are often run on surfaces and terrain that differ significantly from most 100-mile races. As such, the type of specificity training required for 24-hour and 135-mile races is likely to be quite different. Take a look at chapter 3 for more information on specificity.

Training Plan for a 100-Mile Race on 50 Miles per Week

Week	Mon	Tues	Wed	Thurs	Fri	Sat	Sun	Total	Thurs Speed Work Duration
1	Rest	6	5	6	Rest	12	5	34	No speed work
2	Rest	6	5	6	Rest	14	5	36	No speed work
3	Rest	6	5	6	Rest	16	5	38	No speed work
4	Rest	5	3	5	Rest	14	5	32	No speed work
5	Rest	6	5	7	Rest	16	7	41	12-15 mins
6	Rest	6	5	7	Rest	18	7	43	12-15 mins
7	Rest	6	5	7	Rest	18	10	46	15-18 mins
8	Rest	6	4	6	Rest	14	7	37	12-15 mins
9	Rest	7	5	7	Rest	21	5	45	15-18 mins
10	Rest	7	5	7	Rest	14	12	45	15-18 mins
11	Rest	7	5	7	Rest	24	5	48	No speed work
12	Rest	6	5	6	Rest	16	5	38	18-20 mins
13	Rest	7	5	7	Rest	18	7	44	20-25 mins
14	Rest	7	5	3	Rest	**31**	Rest*	46	No speed work
15	Rest*	5	4	7	Rest	14	10	40	20-25 mins
16	Rest	7	5	7	Rest	24	5	48	15-18 mins
17	Rest	7	5	7	Rest	18	14	51	20-25 mins
18	Rest	5	4	7	Rest	14	10	40	20-25 mins
19	Rest	5	Rest	3	Rest	**50**	Rest*	58	No speed work
20	Rest*	6	4	6	Rest	14	5	35	No speed work
21	Rest	7	Rest	7	Rest	24	14	52	20-25 mins
22	Rest	5	5	7	Rest	18	Rest	35	18-20 mins
23	Rest	5	Rest	7	Rest	10	5	27	12-15 mins
24	5	Rest	4	Rest	2	**100**	Rest	109	No speed work

Shading indicates a recovery or taper week.
Bold indicates a race.
Note: You can substitute a 100k race for the 50 miler in week 19.
* Active Recovery is particularly important on this day!

Training Plan for a 100-Mile Race on 70 Miles per Week

Week	Mon	Tues	Wed	Thurs	Fri	Sat	Sun	Total	Thurs Speed Work Duration
1	Rest	7	5	7	Rest	12	6	37	No speed work
2	Rest	7	6	7	Rest	14	6	40	12-15 mins
3	Rest	8	6	8	Rest	16	6	44	12-15 mins
4	Rest	7	5	7	Rest	14	5	38	No speed work
5	Rest	8	6	8	Rest	18	8	48	15-18 mins
6	Rest	8	6	8	Rest	18	12	52	15-18 mins
7	Rest	10	6	8	Rest	20	10	54	18-20 mins
8	Rest	8	5	7	Rest	14	6	40	12-15 mins
9	Rest	10	6	8	Rest	20	12	56	18-20 mins
10	Rest	12	6	10	Rest	16	14	58	20-25 mins
11	Rest	14	6	8	Rest	24	10	62	18-20 mins
12	Rest	10	6	8	Rest	16	10	50	20-25 mins
13	Rest	14	6	10	Rest	18	14	62	18-20 mins
14	Rest	10	6	4	Rest	31	Rest*	51	No speed work
15	Rest*	8	6	10	Rest	16	10	50	20-25 mins
16	Rest	12	6	10	Rest	24	12	64	20-25 mins
17	Rest	12	6	10	Rest	22	20	70	No speed work
18	Rest*	10	6	12	Rest	16	10	54	20-25 mins
19	Rest	10	6	4	Rest	50	Rest*	70	No speed work
20	Rest*	5	6	10	Rest	16	12	49	No speed work
21	Rest	10	8	8	Rest	24	20	70	20-25 mins
22	Rest	10	6	10	Rest	20	5	51	18-20 mins
23	Rest	8	5	8	Rest	10	5	36	15-18 mins
24	5	Rest	4	Rest	2	100	Rest	111	No speed work

Shading indicates a recovery or taper week.
Bold indicates a race.
Note: You can substitute a 100k race for the 50 miler in week 19.
* Active Recovery is particularly important on this day!

Quick Reference Guide:

This table indicates where crucial information regarding the training plan can be found.

Subject	Page(s)
Active recovery	47, 52-4
Back-to-back (B2B) long runs	35-6
Long runs	33-4
Modification of training plan—general	80-85
Speed work	37-46
Training for course specifics	61-73, 76-7

7

TRAIL RUNNING BASICS

This book is about ultramarathons, not trail running. However, a majority of ultras are run on trails these days. The following chapter highlights a few of the differences and challenges encountered while trail running. In particular, you'll learn how the trails affect your speed and stride, why walking makes sense in trail running, what dangers you may face along the trail, what to do when nature calls, and, in a concluding essay, how to take care of the trails you run. For a full guide to trail running, I highly recommend Adam Chase and Nancy Hobbs's *Ultimate Guide to Trail Running*, second edition.

Life's Crooked Paths

I've been running trails as long as I've been running. Given the choice between running on a road or a trail, I'd choose the trail nearly every time. In part, that's because trails often lead to adventure, to serenity, and to nature. However, in my mind, even the "trail" along the edge of a one-block city park is a step up from the concrete sidewalk a few feet away. That leads me to think that the constant variability of trails is one thing that draws me to them.

Variability is one of the defining characteristics of trails. You will need to acknowledge this variability in how you run. That means adapting both your stride and your mental approach.

Negotiating the rocks, roots, and other obstacles on a trail requires more awareness than your average road run. However, don't fear the trail, and avoid tensing up. Tensing up only increases the chance of injury when you misstep. If you stay relaxed, you are more likely to roll through any miscues or to avoid them altogether. If you are initially apprehensive about running trails, gradually introduce yourself to more difficult terrain. There's no need to go run a boulder-strewn mountainside your first time out there.

Shortening your stride helps you avoid obstacles, as you have more opportunities to navigate around them. Shorter strides also keep you from overcommitting. When you overcommit with a long stride, it's harder to float your stride a bit longer to clear an obstacle.

For safety's sake, become vigilant in observing your surroundings as you trail run. In road running, you can often look far off into the distance and zone out. Both are invitations to fall while trail running.

Trails require you to focus your gaze on the ground closer to you than when you're road running. The more technical (difficult to negotiate due to obstacles) the terrain, the closer you have to focus your gaze. On the other hand, you don't want to be looking at your feet. Look at the ground a few strides ahead to anticipate and plan future footfalls. As you grow more comfortable with trail running, you may find that you can focus your gaze farther down the trail.

The predictability of road running often allows us to zone out. In fact, sometimes road running seemingly requires it. However, I often end up disgustedly reminding myself to pay attention after a stumble or fall while trail running. Rather than increasing confidence, an easy or familiar trail can lull a trail runner into complacency. All it takes is an extra inch of rock or root to shatter that complacency. Music, daydreaming, frustration about a mishap, or merely passing or getting passed by another person can take away focus and lead to some time on the ground.

Trail running also requires a few mental shifts in thinking about time. For the most part, there's little variation in pace between and during non-speed-work road runs. You get used to running a pace.

If you run 30 seconds per mile slower than usual, you may suspect you're fatigued or getting sick, while running a standard loop 15 seconds per mile faster than usual might be a breakthrough. It's best to throw such pace-based expectations out the window when you hit the trail. Any number of factors can slow your pace significantly.

The sometimes slower pace of trails just means more time to enjoy the scenery. (Photo by PatitucciPhoto.com)

With few exceptions, trails are slower than roads. Even well-packed dirt absorbs more energy than asphalt or cement. Rocks, roots, and the occasional downed tree require you to shift your momentum. Sand and loose gravel reduce traction and your speed. So, too, does weather-induced mud, snow, or ice. There's also a great deal more variability in pitch on trails than on roads, so you're much more likely to encounter stiff climbs. When you couple a steep hill with poor footing or high elevation, pace slows even more. Adding an extra few pounds of water, food, and gear also does nothing to help your pace. That's okay. Accept that your pace will be slower on trails than on roads. Minute for minute, you get just as good a workout as you do on the roads—and you might just find yourself willing to spend more time running the trails than the roads. That means a better overall endurance workout.

Walking, Your New Best Friend*

Think walking is anathema to trail running? You're wrong. It's all a matter of degrees. Even the world's best trail runners walk when the terrain, slope, and distance dictate they do so. And we're not just talking about ultramarathons. For instance, during the 12-kilometer 2010 World Mountain Running Championships, Max King, the second American on the silver-winning US team, "didn't walk much, but there was a steep two-mile section of which I walked probably 10 percent. I never like to [walk], but sometimes it just makes sense."

As humans, we have two primary forms of bipedal locomotion: running and walking. As a general rule, walking is more energy-efficient at slower speeds, while running is more efficient at faster speeds. This principle does not change when we start charging up a hill. The constant tug of gravity does, however, reduce the speed at which the transition from running to walking occurs—for two reasons.

First, there's the physics of the two modes of travel while gravity is pulling us down. Running is essentially a series of bounds separated by a moment of suspension. During the suspension phase, gravity accelerates us downward, which results in a "tall" parabolic arc with an increased vertical component. We use significant energy to launch ourselves into the suspension phase against the pull of gravity. On the other hand, walking lacks a moment of suspension. Instead, we travel in a series of "flatter" circular arcs. When we run up a hill, we need to exaggerate the height of the flight phase, while there is no flight phase to exaggerate when walking uphill. Krissy Moehl, winner of the mountainous Hardrock 100 and Ultra-Trail

* This section is adapted from the article "Walk, Don't Run: How Walking Uphill Can Speed Up Your Trail Runs" that I wrote for the March 2011 issue of *Trail Runner* magazine.

du Mont-Blanc, succinctly crystallized this concept: "Walking takes the bouncing out of your stride."

Second, as a hill's gradient increases, so will the effort required to run up it. In longer races, the effort needed to run a particular incline may exceed the average effort a runner will optimally expend during the race and, therefore, burn through fuel stores too fast. In shorter races, it might simply be impossible to continue running up a steep pitch.

Before figuring out when you should walk while trail running, you must first decide that you are willing to walk. This might be more difficult for runners who have primarily run shorter distances or who have come from a road running background. Know that you're not swallowing your pride when you walk. You're simply taking part in an activity that includes both running and walking.

Once you have embraced (or at least accepted) the idea of walking while trail running, you need to decide when to walk. Look for two clues. To start, if your breathing is ragged, that's an excellent sign that you should be walking. In addition, unless you're nearing the finish, if you're running up a hill and everyone around you is walking, take a hint from them. Tonya Olson, an ultrarunner and physical therapist, shares a lesson she learned early in her ultrarunning career: "If everyone experienced in a sport is engaging in an activity, then maybe you should, too."

As you gain experience with walking during trail runs, you should build awareness of what perceived effort you can or want to exert throughout an entire outing. If you try to maintain an even effort on the ups, flats, and, downs, you'll know to downshift from running to walking up a hill when your effort goes much above your target. Obviously, this target effort tends to be harder in racing than in training and harder in shorter runs than in longer ones.

Indeed, in increasingly long ultras, runners will mix walking into flat stretches and even into descents. For some, running a regimented time-based run–walk pattern makes sense from the gun. They know they can't run the entire way and acknowledge that a

Galloway marathon approach will serve them well in the long haul. For most, the final half of a 100-miler involves significant stretches of walking. This walking is often more out of necessity than design.

So when does Max King switch to walking? "If I figure out that walking is just as fast as running, then it's pointless not to walk." That makes sense when running uphill, but don't forget the ultra-running adage, "If it hurts to walk and it hurts to run, then run!"

Lean on Me: Get a Boost From Trekking Poles*

European trail runners long ago accepted the use of trekking poles during mountainous outings. Americans were slow to adopt poles, but are using them with increasing frequency. Trekking poles are most useful when climbing. It's easy to envision a runner on a steep trail, stooped over with hands on knees in an attempt to recruit his or her arms for propulsion. Now imagine a pole-planting runner gaining those upper-body strength benefits without bending over. Some runners also find that poles promote a quicker, more efficient cadence when climbing.

Krissy Moehl won the 2009 Ultra-Trail du Mont-Blanc, a highly mountainous 103-mile race through the Alps, using poles for the first time in a race. When asked if poles helped, she replied, "Definitely! I cranked on those things, especially in the later miles. There were three significant climbs in the last 30 miles, and I was able to really pull on the poles."

In a longer race, not only could the increased climbing rate help your time, but the poles could leave you with more in the tank late in the race. After the Leadville 100, ultramarathon veteran Garett Graubins said, "I think they saved my legs just a tiny bit with each step. And, during a 100-mile race, that sort of molecular-level conservation can really add up."

* This section is adapted from the article "Run Quietly and Carry Two Big Sticks: Trekking Poles Take Off with Trail Runners" that I wrote for the June 2010 issue of *Trail Runner* magazine.

How to Walk Uphill

Even though you walk around every day, you may still have something to learn about walking uphill. The most common mistake is climbing with the wrong muscles. Physical therapist Tonya Olson states, "You should push yourself up with your glutes, rather than pull yourself up the mountain with your quads and calves." Not only will you be using a bigger set of muscles when you need them most, you'll be resting other muscles for farther on down the trail.

To help engage your glutes (aka your butt), lean slightly forward with your center of mass slightly in front of your pelvis. Olson suggests, "Lean into the hill to the extent that you feel yourself engaging your glutes." However, you don't want to hunch over. Be sure to keep your back straight.

Once you are using your glutes, focus on shortening your stride and maintaining an even cadence. Long strides with a large moment of suspension are a big energy waster, as they require greater effort to overcome the pull of gravity. Foot placement should be such that when you look down, your line of sight falls even with your toes.

Consider using trekking poles while walking up extremely steep or long climbs, particularly in marathon or longer events. They can help you power up a hill. In contrast, you don't want to use your hands on your knees while you're climbing, as that's a sign you're engaging your quads rather than your glutes.

What's the single best way to improve your walking uphill? Practice walking uphill. Otherwise, Olson advises trying any activity or exercise that isolates the glutes, such as side-lying hip abduction, a single leg bridge, or a split squat with your rear foot elevated.

This essay is adapted from the article "Walk, Don't Run: How Walking Uphill Can Speed Up Your Trail Runs" that I wrote for the March 2011 issue of Trail Runner *magazine.*

Trekking poles provide a big boost in the mountains. (Photo by author)

Don't necessarily put the poles away before heading down a steep or technical trail. They enhance both downhill stability and confidence, not to mention taking the strain off blown quads or a tweaked knee. As a bonus, an expert user slaloms down switchbacks by pushing off the outside of the turn with a pole.

Adverse terrain and conditions can also warrant using poles. For instance, they can add stability when crossing a stream or skirting a puddle, and provide extra traction in mud and slippery conditions. Germany's Hans Dieter Weisshaar, finisher of around 50 100-milers using trekking poles, recently stopped using them, and dropped out of the 2009 McNaughton 100. "It was mud, mud, mud, thick and creamy and slippery," said Weisshaar. "Most likely with poles I would have finished."

There are some downsides to running with trekking poles. For instance, a pole can turn into a skewer if you trip and fall on a pointy grip or stab yourself in the lower leg. Toting unused trekking poles (some runners prefer not to use them on flats or descents) can be awkward. If you carry them in one or both hands, you're not free to hold water bottles, eat gels, or snap photos from a ridgetop. Otherwise, you've got to figure out how to stow them in or on a pack you're wearing.

If you run with trekking poles, first adjust the poles to the correct height. With your arm at your side, bend it to 90 degrees at the elbow and adjust the pole so your forearm is parallel to the ground while you're holding the handle.

Phil Villeneuve, a Nordic skier who also uses poles while running, gives the following advice on climbing technique: "Maximize efficiency by synchronizing opposite foot and pole strikes and pushing/pulling back at the same time. It should feel like a natural motion. The poles should be planted even with or slightly behind the foot. The hips should be forward, with the chest and head up. There should be no (or very little) bend at the hips." He adds that, initially, you should expect sore triceps, biceps, and shoulders the next day.

Remember to be courteous when using poles and be aware that some trail races bar their use, such as the Western States and Angeles Crest 100-milers.

Staying Safe on the Trails

While out on the trails, you will encounter situations that you are unlikely to have encountered on the roads as well as familiar situations with unfamiliar consequences. The purpose of the following section is to make you aware of these differences rather than to scare you. So long as you are aware and respectful of your surroundings, the risks are on par with road running.

The primary safety difference between road and trail running is the reduced likelihood of immediate help. In all but the most frequently traveled urban trails, you should be prepared to spend at least a few hours longer than planned in that environment. It's easy enough to imagine severely spraining an ankle and having to hobble back to the trailhead. While the same ankle sprain could easily happen stepping on or off a curb in a city, you'll get fast help there via a passerby or phoned-for assistance.

In general, don't rely on a cell phone to guarantee assistance. Steep canyons, an errant hill, or poor coverage (as well as a dead battery or water damage) can quickly negate a phone's usefulness. Even if you know that the entirety of your route has reliable cell service, it could be quite a long time before assistance can reach you. As a fail-safe, provide a friend or family member with your route and your expected return time for both your intended and "bad day" scenarios.

Now that you're aware that you might be spending some unintended quality time on the trail, it's time to think of your basic needs: food, water, and shelter.

It's always wise to pack a bit more food than you predict you'll need with the safety margin increasing with the length of your run. While you're not likely to starve on the trail, having a few extra hundred calories can mean the difference between you running yourself out of the woods and a slow trudge as conditions deteriorate.

How to Fall

If you spend much time trail running, it's only a matter of time before you fall. Here are some tips to minimize the damage when you do fall.

1. **Speed up.** Why not avoiding hitting the ground if you can? Catching a toe is a frequent cause of falls. After catching a toe, try accelerating your foot turnover to run your way out of falling. Even if you do eventually hit the ground, you'll have increased the chances of a gradual "Superman" fall as opposed to a full-on face plant.

2. **Survey the scene.** Hopefully, you've been watching the trail and have spotted dangerous obstacles. If not, you may have a split second to see if you're in danger of hitting something hard. Take note, quickly.

3. **Avoid rocks and hard places.** If you're crashing toward a hard object, do what you can to keep your head, chest, and knees, in that order of priority, from hitting it.

4. **Relax.** Once a face-first impact with forgiving ground is unavoidable, relax. You'll likely do more harm than good sticking an arm straight out. Keep your hands close to your body with your palms out to keep your head from hitting the ground first.

5. **Roll with it.** In the fortunate situation that you are crashing into obstacle-free singletrack, try rolling with it, literally. Tuck one shoulder and pull off a somersault. You did them as kids and you can do them again.

As discussed in the next chapter, dehydration impacts perform-ance and threatens your health. That's why if you're going for a long run on trails you should bring excess water, especially where water sources will not be present; bring a water purification method; or be willing to drink from an untreated water source should a desperate need arise. Drinking untreated water can lead to numerous unpleas-ant illnesses, so avoid it when possible.

When trail running, clothing is your shelter, so there's no need to learn how to build a survival shelter before heading out for a trail run. However, before hitting the trail, know the forms and likeli-hood of inclement weather for that region, altitude, and season. Then imagine having to sit unmoving in that weather for 12 hours, and pack what you need to survive. You don't necessarily have to pack clothes to be comfortable, but you do have to survive. Keep in mind the possibility of quickly dropping temperatures, high winds, and precipitation. If you can handle a couple of hours in a low-elevation summer thunderstorm in a T-shirt and shorts, then no extra clothing is needed. On the other hand, mountain thunder-storms can drop temperatures from pleasant to dangerous in minutes. If these conditions may be encountered, bring at least a wind jacket, if not a waterproof shell to throw on as soon as the rain starts falling. On long runs in cold weather, it's imperative to have clothing to keep you warm if you are reduced to a walk.

While on the subject of weather, remember that heat is just as deadly as cold. If you'll be running in hot weather, brush up on the signs of and remedies for heat exhaustion and heatstroke. When rel-evant, monitor yourself for these signs and be prepared to react. Dur-ing a double crossing of the Grand Canyon, I became aware that my heart rate was much higher than what it should have been for the steady decline I was running. I was experiencing tachycardia, one symptom of heat exhaustion. To remedy the situation, I sat for 20 minutes in a cool stream. One pleasant soak later, my heart rate had returned to normal and I was able to continue on my way.

A cool morning is no warning for scorching afternoon temperatures, especially in the Grand Canyon. (Photo by author)

When you're out on the trails, educate yourself about your surroundings. Aside from local weather risks, brush up on the local flora and fauna.

In general, plants present little more than an annoyance. Plants with thorns and needles are self-evident dangers, which you'll surely try to avoid. Irritant plants, such as poison ivy, poison oak, poison sumac, and stinging nettles, are not so conspicuous, but annoying once you realize you've touched them. Learn to identify the local nuisances and then avoid brushing against them. If you frequently run in an environment with poison ivy, oak, or sumac, develop a plan for cleaning yourself, gear, and clothing after running through the woods.

Most wild animals avoid humans when given the chance, so give them the chance to do so. As with plants, learn which wild animals pose the biggest threats, how to avoid encounters with these animals, and what to do if you do run into them. There are few general rules that apply to all animals, aside from giving them plenty of space. In addition, don't provoke them and don't mess with their young. If you encounter a large predatory mammal, it's generally a bad idea to run away, because that triggers their hunting response. Do not underestimate the ability of large herbivores to hurt you. Moose, elk, deer, javelinas, and even cows can inflict serious bodily harm. Getting away from a large herbivore is almost always a good idea, especially when you can change directions a few times, darting back and forth. Don't be frightened if you learn you will be running in venomous snake territory. Instead, learn what the relevant snakes look like as well as when and where you're most likely to encounter them. After that, all you have to do is keep a keen eye on the trail. Unless you're prone to anaphylactic shock, insects in the United States represent little more than an annoyance while running.

Does a Bear **** in the Woods?

Eventually, running the trails means going to the bathroom in the great outdoors. This may cause trepidation among some runners, so I've included some advice on going about your business. My primary suggestion is to be courteous to others. If you plan on bringing wiping paper on your run, I recommend paper towels over toilet paper—they hold up better when subjected to perspiration or wet environments.

For Men

Guys, chances are you've been urinating outside for most of your life. Even if you haven't, don't be anxious. So long as you attempt to be discreet, peeing in the wilderness is widely accepted. On a training run, pull off the side of the trail in a location where cover obscures your front, but where you can see at least a few dozen yards down the trail in both directions. Having these sight lines allows you to turn your body away if you see someone approaching rather than being caught by surprise. In a race, head to the side of the trail and urinate off the trail while facing primarily in the direction of travel, but skewed 15 or 20 degrees off the trail so you shield runners as they pass by. During races, some men attempt to urinate while walking or running. This is a skill acquired with practice; it can be mess, and it's not always much faster than a quick pit stop.

For Women

You should know that it's okay for women to urinate outdoors and even to do so in a setting as public as a trail race. How you urinate on the trail is dictated by what you're wearing. If you have on tights or compression shorts, then step to the side of the trail and turn to face the direction you came from, or step off the trail into cover and turn to face the trail, skewing slightly in the direction from which you came. From there, it's time to squat. Note that squatting can be difficult on tired legs late in an ultra. If you're wearing running shorts or a skirt with a brief, then you could instead step to the side of the trail and face the direction you're headed while skewed slightly off the trail, or step off the trail into cover and turn to face the trail, skewing slightly in the direction toward which you're headed. Spread your legs shoulder width or slightly farther apart, pull the briefs to the side, and urinate standing up. Of course, if you're sporting a bottom with a brief, you can still use the squat method as described for the tights wearer.

Defecating in the Woods

Once you've got an urge that warrants the use of a portable toilet, there's little going back. To lessen the likelihood of that urge during a race, try limiting the amount of fiber in your lunch and dinner the day preceding the race. For an ultra, plan ahead by carrying two or three loperamide tablets (Imodium AD). Then, if you feel a bout of diarrhea coming on, try popping a pair to at least limit the number of bathroom breaks.

When the urge is irresistible, discretion is key. First and foremost, get off the trail. Try to find an easily accessible barrier 5 or 10 yards off the trail. While facing the trail, make use of the down-trail side of the barrier so that it acts as a screen to oncoming runners. If no barrier is available, head at least 10 yards off the trail, put whatever cover you can find between you and oncoming runners, and face back up the trail you just ran down, perhaps turning 30 degrees toward the trail. It's far better that other runners see your embarrassed face than the alternative.

Ideally, adhere to Leave No Trace principles that call for you to "Deposit solid human waste in catholes dug 6 to 8 inches deep at least 200 feet from water, camp, and trails. Cover and disguise the cathole when finished." These principles also call for you to pack out toilet paper. In the heat of a race, few follow Leave No Trace,* but courtesy remains paramount. Moving a rock or small log will create a small receptacle for your waste. After taking care of business, replace the object while being certain to fully cover all toilet paper in a manner that assures it never blows away.

* Please take the time to dig a rudimentary cathole in especially delicate environments, such as in deserts or above tree line. In such places, waste is slow to degrade and toilet paper may last for decades.

Protect-A-Place, for the Places You Want to Protect Most: A New and Improved Formula for Running Trails Responsibly

Dakota Jones

Hey there! Have you ever been hurt by development? Have some of your favorite places in the world been cut down by uncaring human expansion? Well, worry no longer! Science estimates that way too much open space has been filled with irresponsible development in the past 50 years alone, and humans are showing no signs of stopping soon. But that doesn't mean *you can't stop them yourself!* Try Protect-A-Place! It's responsible trail running in a can. Guaranteed to remove any development within 100 yards, or you can just do it yourself! It'll keep the places you like best, like the places you like best.

We've all been there: A pleasant day running along a mountain trail when you round a bend and all of a sudden *bam!* a big ol' road in the way. In the past you might have accepted this blow and kept running. But no longer! With Protect-A-Place you don't have to just sit idly by while the Man bulldozes your wilderness! All you have to do is open up an affordable can of Protect-A-Place and watch your Place get Protected!

Protect-A-Place was founded in 2004 by a group of friends dedicated to saving our wildlands. One day while running in Colorado they came across a brand-new condominium development being installed right on the side of a mountain! Clearly this had to go, so they spent the next several weeks working in a garage in Telluride. The end result was Protect-A-Place, the world's first ever productive-activism in a can! Protect-A-Place uses a unique formula that, when exposed to air, reacts with any unnecessary development happening within 100 yards and wipes the place clean. Just like running eliminates poor fitness, so Protect-A-Place eliminates poor decisions*!

But what exactly does Protect-A-Place do? It utilizes the finest in environmental management techniques to render a place degraded by human development whole once again. Whether it's a road, development, or a coal-fired power plant, Protect-A-Place can reshape a landscape into the healthy ecosystem it once was. Listed below are the active ingredients, all of which are all organic, all-natural, free-trade-certified, hippie-approved, and can actually be useful to runners while out on the trail themselves.

Ingredients in Responsible Trail Running

1. **Stay on the trail.** Trails are ecologically friendly ways to see the backcountry. They generally take the smartest course through an area and, as a result, are used by wildlife as well as people. Cutting switchbacks or running off-trail is decidedly lame and degrades the landscape by encouraging others to follow in your footsteps. Stay on the trail to maintain the beauty of the area.

2. **Don't litter.** This should be unnecessary to say, because *everybody* knows littering sucks. For so many reasons, too. Littering degrades the landscape, injures the wildlife, takes away from the experience of others, and just looks really bad. The rule is to pack out what you pack in, and for runners that's simple enough. Not littering extends to human waste, which should be buried 6 to 8 inches deep to avoid contamination. Staying conscious of what we carry allows us to protect our favorite areas.

3. **Be friendly.** Of course you are anyway, but being friendly makes other people want to work with you. By keeping the trails amicable, runners boost the goodwill of other users and make the trails a worthy use of resources for government planners.

4. **Plan ahead and prepare.** Making sure you know where you're going and what you're going to encounter is often the

---

*This does not include those decisions resulting in loss of money, personal injuries, or children. Only poor environmental stewardship.

difference between a fun day of running and a hideous epic of painful torment. Search-and-rescue is costly, disrupts wildlife, and consumes a lot of resources. Tell someone where you're going and prepare adequately.

5. **Run in small groups.** Keeping group sizes down reduces overall impact on a trail and the area at large. Small groups don't disturb wildlife as readily or erode the trail quite as quickly and are, therefore, much more conducive to a healthy environment.

6. **Leave what you find.** Not that runners are in a position to pack out rocks and sticks and such, but sometimes an object surfaces that is just too perfect to be left behind. Well, *leave it behind.* In most cases, things are where they are for a reason, and moving them disrupts their purpose. An important exception to this rule is litter, in which case you should refer back to rule 2.

Other ingredients are force, patience, and a lot of earth-moving equipment, but that's why you have this great product! Protect-A-Place is the environmentalist's answer to development. It's what people who want to make the world a healthier, altogether more runnable place use to save the areas they love. Protect-A-Place is recognized worldwide as the standard for wilderness reclamation, so why can't it work for you? Log onto our website and order your Protect-A-Place so you can take back your wilderness! And remember, if this turns out to be completely fake, don't just give up, make your own Protect-A-Place! It's fast, it's fun, and it can even save the planet!

Protect-A-Place—For the Places You Want to Protect Most!

Dakota Jones is a standout ultrarunner who proved himself before the age of 20 with a near-course-record win at the 2010 San Juan Solstice 50-mile and a fourth-place finish at the 2010 The North Face Endurance Challenge 50-mile championships.

8

HYDRATION AND ELECTROLYTES: KEEPING THE GLASS HALF FULL

Staying hydrated is paramount to success in an ultramarathon. Just a 2 or 3 percent loss in body weight from sweating can result in a 10 percent drop-off in endurance performance. Marathoners may be familiar with the concept of cardiac drift, which results when dehydration decreases blood volume, leading to a reduction in oxygenated blood flow. The net result of cardiac drift is a slow upward trend in heart rate while the runner maintains an even effort. Cardiac drift is

Failing to properly hydrate is an unnecessary mistake.
(Photo by PatitucciPhoto.com)

worsened by hot conditions that draw blood from the muscles to the skin to assist with cooling.

Beyond endurance performance reductions, dehydration can also lead to cramps, digestion issues, and blisters. Extreme dehydration can lead to life-threatening as well as chronic health conditions. In other words, it's best to stay hydrated on the long run. To hydrate properly, you need to know how much you sweat, how to balance water and electrolytes, how to monitor your hydration, and how to drink on the run.

Fluid Loss

Unless you know how much you sweat, it's impossible to maintain proper hydration. Sweat rate varies based on many environmental factors. For instance, temperature, relative humidity, and altitude all affect the rate at which you sweat. So, too, does the effort with which you are running.

The most effective way to measure sweat rate is to conduct a sweat test on yourself. To do this, weigh yourself completely naked before going out for a run of 60 to 90 minutes in length. After weighing yourself, do not eat, drink, or use the bathroom until you've completed your run, at which time reweigh yourself completely naked. After your post-run weigh-in, calculate the difference between your starting and finishing weight. Each pound you lost during the sweat test represents 16 ounces of sweat. Divide the total number of ounces lost to sweating during the test by the number of minutes you ran. Multiply this number by 60 to determine your sweat rate in number of ounces per hour.

Keep in mind that sweat rate varies markedly depending on the exact environmental conditions and level of exertion. Therefore, you may want to conduct multiple sweat tests to determine your sweat rate under a variety of conditions. In particular, if you are determining your hydration rate with a particular goal race in mind, conduct the sweat test under conditions that mimic likely race conditions as closely as possible.

As you gain experience, you'll likely be able to estimate how much fluid you should be consuming in various situations. No matter how much you are sweating, it's difficult for the body to process much more than 24 to 28 ounces of water per hour.

Electrolytes and Hydration

During long bouts of exercise, be sure to take in electrolytes. In fact, it's crucial to maintain a proper balance between water and electrolyte intake—this balance plays an important role in muscle, digestive, and other bodily systems.* Electrolytes include water-soluble ions such as sodium, potassium, calcium, magnesium, and chloride. Each of these electrolytes is shed from the human body in sweat. While modern diets provide sufficient amounts of these minerals for less active individuals, sweat loss from prolonged exercise easily results in short-term electrolyte deficiencies when insufficient amounts of electrolytes are consumed during exercise.

Replacing sodium is important once you start replacing fluids during runs, and it becomes crucial as the length of the run approaches ultra distances. In warm weather it's typical to consume 400mg of sodium** per hour, while 800mg or more may be prudent in hot weather. Potassium loss is small enough that the consumption of a sports drink or electrolyte tablet to replace sodium provides the necessary potassium. I will leave the debate as to which other electrolytes are necessary during exercise up to the various sports drink and electrolyte manufacturers. The highly variable inclusion or exclusion of electrolytes other than sodium and potassium suggests a lack of scientific consensus on the subject.

---

* The most dangerous hydration–electrolyte imbalance, dilutional hyponatremia, is caused by overhydrating while consuming insufficient electrolytes. See the Water–Electrolyte Balance table (page 127) for more information regarding the symptoms and treatment of dilutional hyponatremia.

** The given amounts are expressed for sodium. This equates to 1 to 2 grams of sodium chloride, aka table salt.

The three most common ways to replenish electrolytes while running are through sports drinks, food, and dietary supplements. Each of these means of electrolyte replacement varies significantly in terms of the types and quantity of electrolytes. With that in mind, it's easiest to focus on one or two primary sources of electrolytes during a particular run. Often these sources are a sports drink and electrolyte tablets. However, even if you focus on these two sources, don't turn a blind eye if you consume significant amounts of sodium from other sources such as broth, snack foods, or salted potatoes commonly found at ultras.

Electrolyte-containing sports drinks are the most familiar way for an athlete to replenish electrolytes on the go. Most often, these sports drinks are available in pre-mixed or powder form. In recent years, effervescent tablets and concentrated packets have been added to the sports drink repertoire. These new-format sports drinks are often calorie-free. The wide range of sodium (50 to 200mg) and potassium (15 to 100mg) content per 8-ounce serving can make it difficult to calculate your exact electrolyte intake from beverages. Therefore, I recommend relying on electrolyte tablets even if you are hydrating with sports drink, but adjusting for the sports drink's electrolyte content by taking the electrolyte tablets less frequently than recommended. You should be able to handle a slight excess in electrolytes. Review the water–electrolyte balance table for guidance regarding further details on hydration and electrolyte replacement.

While electrolyte supplementation, whether in the form of a beverage, food, or a pill, works well for many runners, there are two ways that you can reduce your electrolyte requirements. First, reduce the amount of electrolytes and, in particular, sodium in your diet. It has been shown that over time, a low-sodium diet can lower the concentration of sodium in sweat, which means you require less sodium intake during exercise. Second, regular exposure to high temperatures reduces the concentration of sodium in sweat. The greatest reduction is seen in those who were not previously heat-acclimated.

Hydration: HIGH **Electrolytes HIGH** **Hypernatremia + overhydration** **Likelihood: Very rare** *Symptoms:* * Weight is up a few pounds or more * Thirst is high; salty foods taste bad * Possible mental confusion * Hands may be puffy * Shortness of breath, rapid heart rate * Food acceptance is poor *Causes:* Overconsumption of salt, probably from a combination of sources *What to do:* Stop electrolyte intake. Drink only to wet mouth until weight is normal.	**Hydration: OK** **Electrolytes HIGH** **Hypernatremia** **Likelihood: Rare, transitory if water available** *Symptoms:* * Weight is normal * Thirst is high; salty foods taste bad * Mouth is not very dry *Causes:* No access to water, or voluntary restriction of water intake; body electrolytes concentrated by loss of water *What to do:* Drink water to satisfy thirst, so that excess electrolytes are removed by sweating and urination. Restrict salt intake until excess is urinated and sweated out.	**Hydration: LOW** **Electrolytes HIGH** **Hypernatremia + dehydration** **Likelihood: Moderate** *Symptoms:* * Weight is down a few pounds or more * Thirst is high, salty foods taste bad * Mouth and skin are dry * Food acceptance is poor * Absence of urination *Causes:* No access to water or voluntary restriction of water intake; body electrolytes concentrated by loss of water *What to do:* Get access to water and drink. Restrict electrolytes until weight is near normal.
Hydration: HIGH **Electrolytes OK** **Overhydrated** **Likelihood: Moderate** *Symptoms:* * Weight is up a few pounds or more * Wrists and hands are probably puffy * Stomach is queasy * Thirst is low, and salty foods taste normal * Mouth is moist—can spit *Causes:* Fluid intake in excess of needs *What to do:* Drink only to wet mouth until weight is near normal.	**Hydration: OK** **Electrolytes OK** **Proper hydration and electrolyte balance** **Likelihood: Common** *Symptoms:* * Weight is stable or slightly down * Stomach is fine; food acceptance is normal * Mouth is moist—can spit; skin is normal * Cramps: none * Urination is normal *Causes:* Proper water and electrolyte intake *What to do:* Continue with hydration and electrolyte practice unless conditions change.	**Hydration: LOW** **Electrolytes OK** **Dehydration** **Likelihood: Common** *Symptoms:* * Weight is down a few pounds or more * Thirst is high, and salty foods taste normal. * Mouth is dry, food acceptance is poor * Skin is dry and may tent if pinched * May have dizziness on standing up * May have cramping * Mental performance may be affected *Causes:* Insufficient fluid intake *What to do:* Drink sports drink with electrolytes, or water.
Hydration: HIGH **Electrolytes LOW** **Hyponatremia + overhydration DANGEROUS!** **Likelihood: Moderate** *Symptoms:* * Weight is up a few pounds or more * Wrists and hands are puffy * Nausea, stomach sloshing, possible vomiting * Thirst is low; salty foods taste good * Athlete may show confusion, odd behavior * Mouth is moist—can spit * Urination may be voluminous and crystal clear *Causes:* Overhydration, insufficient sodium intake *What to do:* Drink only to wet mouth until weight is normal, then correct any sodium deficit.	**Hydration: OK** **Electrolytes LOW** **Hyponatremia** **Likelihood: Mild form is common** *Symptoms:* * Weight is normal * Stomach is queasy, with poor food acceptance * Wrists may be puffy * Salty foods taste good * Thirst is normal * Mouth is moist—can spit * May have cramping *Causes:* Insufficient electrolyte intake *What to do:* Increase electrolyte intake until stomach feels okay.	**Hydration: LOW** **Electrolytes LOW** **Hyponatremia + dehydration** **Likelihood: Rare** *Symptoms:* * Weight is down a few pounds or more * Thirst is high, and salty foods taste good * Mouth is dry, can't spit * May have cramping * Skin is dry and may tent if pinched * May have dizziness on standing up *Causes:* Insufficient drinking, no electrolyte intake *What to do:* Take electrolytes and drink sports drink or water.

Monitoring Hydration

Monitoring your hydration level is difficult, so knowing and staying on top of your hydration needs is important. Relatively frequent urination with clear to light-colored urine is a good sign. However, know that a lack of urination for six or eight hours is not uncommon even among athletes who are staying on top of hydration. Exercise and especially moderate-to-intense exercise decreases urine volume and, therefore, frequency. However, as intensity decreases late in long ultramarathons, it is not unusual for urination frequency to increase at least temporarily.

Do not rely on thirst to determine whether you need to drink during an ultra. During exercise, thirst often lags behind hydration needs, and you do not want to be playing catch up out on the course. On the other hand, if you are thirsty, you'd best start drinking!

One of the best ways to determine on-course hydration is to step on a scale. While it may be a bit much to have your crew carry one around, it's not uncommon for scales to be found at a few aid stations during a 100-mile race. Sometimes it's mandatory for you to weigh in. Other times you will not be required to, but might want to do so for reassurance. To get a useful measurement, weigh yourself in your running clothes and shoes (or something similar) before the race and, on race day, take off any pack or other weighty gear you may be wearing. Keep in mind that scales vary by up to a few pounds, so don't panic if you're drinking well, feel great, but weigh in a few pounds off at one weigh-in.

Hauling Your Hydration Source

Unlike marathons and other road races, it's extremely rare that you will be able to amply hydrate by drinking only at aid stations. That mean's you'll carry your beverage(s) of choice along with you.

There are four primary options for carrying your hydration source. Carry one or two handheld water bottles, which consist of a bottle and a strap assembly that holds the bottle to your hand. If you like drinking from bottles, but prefer to free up your hands, use a waist pack that holds one or two bottles, usually around the back of your waist. Many ultrarunners carry one handheld with a spare bottle or two in a waist pack. Although not frequently seen at the front of a race, some runners prefer the convenience of a backpack with a hydration bladder. (There are also a few waist packs outfitted with hydration bladders.) A fourth variant that is much more common in Europe than in North America is taking a backpack and either attaching up to two bottles to the shoulder straps or putting them in holsters on the side of the pack's main compartment.

One advantage that carrying multiple bottles has over most hydration bladders is the ability to carry different beverages at the same time.* Frequently, such a combination involves carrying at least one bottle of water in addition to carrying sports drink. The water-only option provides both a fallback if your stomach is not tolerating the sports drink and, in hot weather, a clean option for dousing yourself to cool off.

Be sure to test whichever hydration system you plan on racing with on long runs before race day. A pack that works for someone else may cause you severe chafing or fail to hold your bottles in place. While a bouncing bottle on your waist might not end your day, the annoyance can detract from your performance and your enjoyment.

---

* A small number of hydration bladders are capable of delivering two different beverages from a split bladder with dual tubes.

Tips for Drinking on the Go

As for the drinking itself, here are a few quick tips:

• Drink in small, regular amounts so that you're constantly hydrating yourself and minimizing the likelihood of overfilling your stomach at any one time.

• Avoid drinking on short, steep inclines. No matter how practiced you are at drinking on the move, you're still likely to miss a breath or two when you need them most.

• Do drink up before or at the start of a very long downhill. Your body will be better able to process the fluid while you reduce your running effort. However, don't overdo pre-hill hydration to the point that your stomach sloshes around uncomfortably.

• On days when it's hard to carry enough fluids between aid stations, drink the last of your fluids when you are certain that you're within 10 or 15 minutes of the next station. You'll absorb some of these fluids before the aid station and be able to drink more once you reach it.

• Plan to drink up at aid stations. On hot days this helps maximize fluid intake while reducing the amount of fluids you need to carry. During a 100-miler, I make sure to grab two disposable cups and drink them (or their equivalent) at every aid station at which I stop.

9

FUELING THE FIRE: NUTRITION AND ULTRAS

Taking up the challenge of running an ultra should have little effect on your day-to-day nutrition. Any increase in daily caloric needs due to increased training time can usually be made up by eating more of what you already eat, assuming you already eat a healthy diet. With that in mind, this chapter offers a few notes regarding general nutrition before discussing ultra-long-run nutrition, which differs significantly from marathon and shorter-race nutrition, nausea, and how to fuel for post-run recovery.

General Notes on Nutrition

I am not a dietitian, nor am I the world's healthiest eater, so I'm not going to lecture anyone on what his or her daily diet should look like. Chances are you've found something that works for you and that you like. If you are looking for general nutritional advice, I recommend reading Matt Fitzgerald's *Racing Weight: How to Get Lean for Peak Performance.* Here Fitzgerald offers balanced, well-supported, easy-to-understand dietary advice rather than the next fad diet.

The key takeaway from Fitzgerald's book is not surprising given its title. That is, find and race at your ideal "racing weight." While finding the ideal balance of muscularity and leanness may be a higher mark than many are willing to shoot for, it brings into focus the quickest and often easiest way that many ultrarunners could improve their running—by safely losing weight. If you doubt this, put a 20th of your bodyweight in a backpack and go run a few miles before taking off the pack and running for a few more. The difference in effort and pace will amaze you. Add some hills to the run to help emphasize these differences in effort and pace. This is not a call to start a starvation diet or to lose as much weight as possible, but rather a call for you to consider whether you could lose 5, 10, or more pounds while retaining your muscle mass and staying healthy.

If you are vegetarian, vegan, or on another meat-free diet, rest assured that your diet is unlikely to be a barrier to ultrarunning. Indeed, the ranks of ultrarunners likely include a higher proportion of vegetarians and vegans than does the general population. As someone who's been vegetarian (or extremely low meat) through most of my ultrarunning career, I've never felt my diet was a detriment to my ultrarunning. More important, numerous ultrarunning elites have eaten a vegetarian or even more restrictive meat-free diet while running at the top of their game. For example, Scott Jurek (vegan) won seven Western States 100 titles and set the American 24-hour record, Ellie Greenwood (vegetarian) won the 2010 100k World Championships, Michael Wardian (vegetarian) earned numerous USATF ultradistance national championships, and Michael Arnstein (fruitarian) ran the fourth fastest time in the long history of the JFK 50 mile. All of that said, even with careful dietary monitoring, a small number of meat-free ultrarunners have been unable balance their nutritional needs with intense training and racing schedules.

Vegetarian or not, many of us take dietary supplements. Some take particular vitamin or mineral supplements to address a known deficiency, while the majority of us take vitamin and mineral supplements as a general precautionary measure. I fall into the latter camp, taking a multivitamin daily as well as iron and B-complex supplements a few times each week. So long as you are taking a standard dosage, such vitamin and mineral supplementation may or may not be helpful, but it's unlikely to do harm.

Beyond vital nutrient supplementation, conduct your own research before purchasing other dietary supplements.* All dietary supplements are regulated in the United States; however, enforcement of these regulations is extremely lax. While claims for supplements are required to have scientific substantiation, in reality that substantiation can be minimal to nonexistent. Limited funding generally restricts regulatory enforcement actions to supplements claiming to cure a significant disease or lead to extreme weight loss, those with millions of dollars in annual sales, or those that pose a real public health risk. That's not to say there aren't useful dietary supplements out there. There are. Do your homework to find them. The good news is that, at recommended dosages, the vast majority of dietary supplements will do nothing worse than hurt your pocketbook.

Feed the Habit: Long Run and Race Day Nutrition

In-race marathon nutrition does not necessarily cut it in an ultra or in some preparatory long runs. In a marathon you rely primarily on your body's limited carbohydrate (glycogen) stores** for energy, with fat being the secondary energy source. Eating two or three gels along the way allows you maintain a slightly harder effort, as racing at that harder effort increases the ratio of carbohydrates to fat you burn. However, there are quickly diminishing returns on eating during marathons due, in part, due to blood diversion to deal with digestion.

When you move up from a road marathon to an ultra, even a

---

* By other dietary supplements, I do not mean to include energy gels or sports drinks, which are labeled as dietary supplements. Nor do I include electrolyte supplements, mentioned in chapter 8.

** Glycogen stores can be increased by carbo loading. Primitive carbo loading (say, simply eating a big bowl of pasta the night before a race) is less effective than more sophisticated methods that first call for carbohydrate depletion of up to seven days. The psychological costs (feeling sluggish and unenergetic) of depletion-based carbo loading are likely greater than the benefits. What's more, the positive effects of carbo loading are further minimized in ultras—carbo loading has only been shown to increase performance when carbohydrates are not consumed during the race. As this chapter suggests, failing to consume in-race carbohydrates is a bad choice.

trail 50k, three important things happen. First, your caloric requirements quickly increase with no increase in your available glycogen
stores. This means you need to obtain additional calories from your
own fat stores or from calories ingested during the race. Second, you
run the race at a lower average effort. As a result, you automatically
decrease the ratio of carbohydrates to fat you burn. In other words,
you run on a higher percentage of fat. Finally, the decreased effort
allows your body to more effectively process the calories you ingest
during the race.

In ultras, eat early and often.

Develop a fueling plan that provides for eating at regular intervals. The timing of those intervals begins when the gun goes off. Do
not wait until your stomach is rumbling or you feel yourself bonking. If you wait that long, you can recover, but it will be a long, hard
road. Avoid that road. Lean toward eating smaller, more frequent
snacks. It's less of a jolt on the stomach and provides more even
energy. For example, if you plan on eating a 200-calorie bar for a
given hour, eat half the bar in two sessions 30 minutes apart.

So how much should you eat during an ultra? In general, you
should shoot for between 250 and 400 calories an hour. The exact
amount will depend on your size, your relative ability to digest
foods, your effort, and the temperature, with higher efforts and
temperatures reducing your ability to process food. Experiment and
find how many calories per hour your body can tolerate while running different paces. I've found I can tolerate 150 calories an hour
from sports drinks (about one bottle), and 200 calories an hour
from energy gels or chews, with 100-calorie portions consumed
every half hour. In the last quarter of an ultra, I may increase my
gel/chew intake to three 100-calorie servings taken at 20-minute
intervals.

Most of your calories come from carbohydrates. Many ultrarunners get these carbohydrates from a combination of carbohydrate-
based sports drinks, energy gels, and energy chews, as these calories

are easily digested.* This scenario is particularly common at the front of an ultra field. Do not rely entirely on simple carbohydrates. Instead, consume a mix of both simple and complex carbohydrates to provide a blend of quick and more sustained energy.

Even elites occasionally mix in some "real food." What is "real food"?** Anything that's not primarily a carbohydrate in a liquid or semi-solid state. Ultras are famous for being running buffets with a smorgasbord of real food. At a start, we're talking fare along the lines of candy, chips, pretzels, fruit, and peanut butter and jelly sandwiches.

Aid stations and their volunteers are welcome sights
during ultramarathons. (Photo by Stephan/Gripmaster)

* Always drink at least half a cup of water (or more if it's a sugar-based drink) for each energy gel or 100 calories of energy chews you consume. Otherwise, the high sugar concentration will make it difficult for your stomach to absorb the sugars. Prolonged failure to consume adequate fluids with energy gels or chews can leads to nausea and vomiting.

** *Real food* is an established term in the ultra community. The term in no way relates to real food in the sense of a healthy diet or avoiding overly processed foods. Indeed, some prominent runners who strictly adhere to eating real food in the healthy sense during their daily lives consume highly processed, nutritionally deficient products during the course of an ultramarathon.

A fancy aid station may have homemade soup, grilled cheese sand-wiches, quesadillas, pizza, or even a full hot breakfast waiting for you.

The varied food selection at ultra aid stations correctly suggests that consuming protein and fat is not off the table. In fact, a small amount of protein may improve performance in ultras. Protein can be found in sports drinks that are specially formulated for ultradis-tance endurance events and in many real foods. Limit your protein consumption to no more than 20 percent of your caloric intake on a run. For some, that may be far too much protein. Not to worry; as noted in the preceding paragraph, many ultrarunners consume only carbohydrate-sourced calories during a race. The primary ben-efit of consuming fat during an ultra is satiation of appetite. After hours of eating even large quantities of carbohydrates, it's common for one's stomach to start rumbling. Fat takes care of that.

Real food with significant amounts of protein and, particularly, fat take longer to digest than engineered carbohydrate energy sources. Keep this in mind while racing. If you eat such foods, try to do so 10 or 15 minutes ahead of your next scheduled eating period. When that's not an option, consider taking in some easily digestible carbohydrates along with the protein- or fat-rich food. This is the beauty of a peanut butter and jelly sandwich or a turkey-avocado tortilla roll-up.

Perhaps the most common adage connected to ultrarunning advice is that we are all "an experiment of one." This could not be more true than with food. What works for one runner may not work for another. Indeed, what works for you one race might not work at all in another race. Still, you need to experiment on what mix of calorie sources (carbs, protein, and fat), which type of foods (for carbs, do you prefer gels, sports drink, fruit, grain-based solid foods . . . ?), and then which specific foods (which brands, which flavors, and even which mix of flavors you prefer). Once you figure out your primary plan, have some alternatives in mind that work for you if that primary plan fails. Whatever changes you make to your plan, aim to minimize any prolonged breaks from eating.

All of the nutrition lessons for race day should be applied to training. Unless your previous running has shown you otherwise, it's unlikely that you'll need to consume any calories for a run of less than two or two and a half hours. Your glycogen and fat stores should be more than sufficient. For runs over two and a half hours, start eating on a semi-regular schedule from the beginning of the run. Given that the effort of a training run is likely to be less than that of a race, you require fewer calories per hour and you can get a higher percentage of calories from fat. That means you can back off your caloric intake per hour to perhaps 50 to 75 percent of race day levels. Part of the goal of long runs is to train your body to burn fat, so consider eating even less on some runs . . . with extra calories available in case of a severe bonk.

Note, however, that it would be useful to have a few hard long runs before your focus race, be they self-planned or preparatory races, in which you test out every aspect of your race day nutrition and hydration plan. What works on a three-hour trot may not work when pushing your body for longer periods. Those just making the switch to ultras may want to practice their race day nutrition plan during most or all of their long runs of more than two and a half hours.

Nausea

Like an army, ultrarunners march on their stomachs. As race distance increases, the ability to fuel continuously becomes increasingly vital lest you be reduced to a very long post-caloric bonk walk. Unfortunately, nausea is widespread during ultras, and so are its causes. Below are a few common causes of and solutions for this.

Many runners develop a fueling plan that works great in training only to find themselves retching trailside during a race. The cause? Taking in too many calories for the increased effort of racing, run-

---

* For the record, I'm including your brain among your basal metabolic functions.

ning too hard in high temperatures, or some combination of the two. Aside from basal metabolic functions,* three bodily systems compete for your limited blood flow: your skeletal muscles to run, your digestive system to nourish, and, when hot, your skin to cool. Increasing the blood flow to any one of these systems limits the flow to others, thereby decreasing their function.

Because you need to keep eating and as weather manipulation is rarely an option, your best bet is to slow down, at least temporarily. Even a modest reduction in pace of 30 seconds or a minute per mile for 15 to 30 minutes, or walking on level ground for 5 to 10 minutes, can greatly improve the state of your stomach with minimal time cost. It is far better to lose a minute or two in prevention than many minutes due to continued nausea, repeated vomiting, or the cumulative effect of not eating for a prolonged period.

Dehydration, by itself, can be a persistent cause of severe nausea. This is yet another reason to maintain proper hydration and to promptly address dehydration should it occur.

Poor gastric emptying that results in a sloshy stomach is another cause of ultrarunning nausea. While this, too, can be caused by heat or too strong a pace, it can also come from an imbalance of water intake and either sugars or electrolytes. Therefore, if you find your stomach gradually becoming increasingly full, carefully consider whether you've been properly balancing your water, sugar, and electrolyte intake. If you conclude that you've previously made a mistake, immediately begin to correct it, but do so gradually. For example, if you've overdone it with either electrolytes or sugar, try diluting your sports drink to half strength for an aid station or two.

Slow your pace as described above if you can't determine a cause for your poor gastric emptying. In the end, vomiting is sometimes the best cure for a sloshing stomach—you'll often feel better immediately, and it provides for a clean slate to ingest the right ratios of water and nutrients. Please know that I don't encourage intentional vomiting. This is merely a lesson learned from personal experience.

Runners who rely entirely or nearly entirely on carbohydrate sports drinks, energy gels, and energy chews are particularly susceptible to increased stomach acidity, which leads to a progressive nausea problem. Taking some antacids may help. So may eating alkaline-forming foods. I prefer eating some watermelon.

Although not a cause of nausea per se, a rumbling stomach is uncomfortable and distracting. After a few hours of racing, it is also quite common among the easy carbohydrate crowd. This is where some "real food" containing fat and protein comes in real handy. Just half a peanut butter and jelly sandwich, a wedge or two of watermelon, or a piece of grilled cheese can leave your stomach feeling better for hours to come.

A final tip for nausea: candied ginger. Ginger is commonly recommended by health care professionals to treat nausea from various causes. Medical research supports the use of ginger to reduce nausea in some circumstances.

Fueling for Recovery

Recovery is a key aspect of training. In the food realm, that means consuming calories quickly after a long run, hard workout, or race. The key window for replacing calories is within two hours of finishing a run. It's ideal to refuel as early as possible within that window. The goal is to ingest at least 1.2 grams of carbs per 2.6 pounds (1.2 kilograms) of body weight in the couple of hours after the workout. Match every 4 grams of carbs with around 1 gram of protein for optimal recovery. It's also important to rehydrate during this period. Your urine should be pale yellow or clear within a few hours of exercising. Taking proper care of your body following a tough workout or race will have you feeling better sooner and running stronger in subsequent runs.

NO PAIN, NO GAIN:
DEALING WITH INJURIES
AND OTHER SETBACKS

If you've been running for any length of time, chances are you've dealt with a running-related injury. Maybe you've had an acute injury such as a sprained ankle caused by turning it on a curb or root—or perhaps you've battled a chronic injury such as Achilles tendonitis or plantar fasciitis. Either way, ultra training and racing exposes you to the same injury risks.

Because there's so much great material available on running injuries, this book will not deal with normal aches and -itises common to all runners. Instead, this chapter examines some of the issues that more commonly crop up among ultramarathoners.

To quickly put what follows in perspective, chafing and blistering are frequent, if not routine, problems that ultrarunners face. So, too, are minor dehydration and nutrition issues—discussed in chapters 8 and 9, respectively. With proper post race care, these setbacks are merely uncomfortable, if performance-limiting, experiences. On the other hand, it is extremely rare for an ultrarunner to experience rhabdomyolysis, the mal-effects of anti-inflammatory use, or, as noted in chapter 8, dilutional hyponatremia. While it is imperative to be aware of this latter set of conditions, the (remote) possibility of their occurrence should in no way dissuade you from attempting or running ultramarathons.

Listen to Your Body

Before moving on, I make an emphatic plea to listen to your body in multiple time frames. In the short term, such as in a race, monitoring and responding to your body can reduce unnecessary pain— and perhaps make the difference between finishing or not. In the long term, paying attention to early signs of bodily stress and dealing with them might mean only a few miles missed in training rather than a few weeks or months off due to injury. This lesson is nothing new, but it's one that even the most conscientious runner should be reminded of from time to time.

The Dish on Chafing

Chafing happens, but during ultras it happens more frequently and more painfully than necessary. In case you are one of the fortunate souls who is unfamiliar with chafing, it's the rubbing raw of your skin through the friction of repetitive movement. Chafing can occur anywhere (take my word for it!) that skin-on-skin or skin-on-fabric friction occurs. The most common areas are the inner thighs of both men and women, men's nipples, anywhere a woman's sports bra touches her body, between arms and torsos, and anywhere a waist or shoulder pack rubs against the body. Each of these types of chafing is preventable or minimizable.

Inner thigh chafing is the most common source in ultras. It comes on as irritation, turns into discomfort, and, if ignored, ends up as waddle-inducing pain that will make you scream in your post-run shower. Yeah, it's best avoided. Thankfully, that's easy with some pre-planning. For many, applying an anti-chafing product (such as Bodyglide) to your inner thighs pre-run will prevent most chafing. However, in very long races it would be wise to have the same brand anti-chafing product with your crew or in your drop bags. If anti-chafing products don't stop your thigh chafing, it's time to try compression shorts or tights that keep some combination of your legs and shorts' fabric from rubbing.

More generally, use Bodyglide or another anti-chafing product you prefer on your body's specific friction points.

Whether caused by sweat, precipitation, or a stream crossing, wet clothing is a major source of chafing. The circumstances that cause wet clothing are largely unavoidable, but if chafing is or could be an issue, try keeping the trouble areas as dry as possible and consider changing the relevant piece of clothing.

Only a few things need to be said about men's nipples. First, there's no pride in bloody nipples or easily avoidable pain. Second, applying two Band-Aids or a couple of strips of athletic tape before a long run is all it takes to prevent this condition. That's all.

Nearly all ultrarunners end up wearing a waist or shoulder pack at some point during training or racing. Without any seeming rhyme or reason, these packs can cause chafing. It occurs along any weight-bearing support piece, such as a shoulder strap or waist belt, or where the pack's load bounces against your body, such as the bottom of a weighted shoulder pack against the small of your back. In either case, try adjusting the support straps and, when possible, the load itself to readjust strap pressure and minimize bouncing. If neither of those methods works and you aren't able to switch to another pack mid-run, you may have to suffer a bit in learning by trial and error. After the unfortunate run, make further attempts at adjusting the pack's straps and support structure or invest in another pack. In a pinch where you can't ditch your pack, tape the affected area of skin for temporary relief.

For other chafing issues, apply one or more of the chafing solutions outlined above. That is: Lube it, cover it, or adjust it.

The Agony of De Feet

Every ultrarunner has experienced painful hot spots, blisters, and toenail problems. In fact, depending on race conditions, foot problems may be the leading cause of runner dropouts. Obviously, that makes prevention and treatment of such problems an important tool in the bag of every ultrarunner. As such, some basics of foot care are described below. For full treatment of the subject, I highly recommend John Vonhof's *Fixing Your Feet*. This frequently updated book, along with Vonhof's website, www.fixingyourfeet.com, has guided ultrarunners for more than a decade. Before dealing with specific problems, let's take a quick look at measures to prevent foot problems in the first place.

To begin with, wear well-fitting shoes. The shoe should fit snugly around your heel with little upward movement once it's tied. It should also not be so big that you need to painfully tighten the laces to prevent your foot from slipping when running downhill. On the other hand, the toebox should be roomy enough that you can wiggle your toes as well as leave half an inch between your longest toe and the front of the shoe. It goes without saying that the shoe's interior should not have any rough or irritating spots.

Once you have a well-fitting pair of shoes, take a few more preventive steps to minimize foot discomfort. First, keep debris from entering your shoe by means of gaiters, shoe choice, or running technique. If significant debris does enter your shoe, empty it out unless you're close to the finish or are prepared to deal with the consequences. Second, keep your feet dry through shoe choice, sock choice, and limiting exposure to water. It may be worth changing out of wet shoes and socks during an ultramarathon, but only if your new kicks are likely to stay dry for a significant period of time. Third, wear socks that work for you, whether thick or thin, single-layer or double-layer, mini crew or knee high. Whatever you do, avoid cotton socks, which don't wick away moisture. Finally, take care of your feet by trimming your toenails, tending to cracked skin, and, if you find they coincide with your blister problems, filing away calluses. See the accompanying "Blister Prevention" essay for additional tips, including the utility of maintaining proper hydration.

Blister Prevention

John Vonhof

Blisters are very predictable. Take three elements—moisture, friction, and heat, all common to your feet when you run—and the likelihood of a blister appearing is high. The longer these elements exist on the feet, unattended to, the greater the risk. So what can you do to reduce one or more of these elements?

The first order of business is to recognize that you, and you alone, need to find what will work on your feet. Others can give suggestions, but what works for another may not work for you. What follows is a synopsis of options you need to consider.

The First Line of Blister Defense

There are several blister-reducing options that should be your first level of defense. Proper socks are a key priority. Moisture-wicking socks are available from almost every sock manufacturer, and given a choice should always be picked before an all-cotton sock. Double-layer socks offer an inner layer that moves against the outer layer, reducing friction to the skin. Try several different types of socks of various thicknesses and fabrics.

Lubricants are next on the list. While it was once common for runners to use Vaseline or Bag Balm as a foot lubricant, most are now using newer, state-of-the-art lubricants that may contain silicone, pain-relieving benzocaine, or anti-friction polymers. The trick with lubricants is to reapply them frequently, being sure to clean off the old layer before another application. If your skin becomes too tender from the softening effects of the lubricant, then a powder may be in order.

Powders can help reduce friction by absorbing moisture. This reduces friction between the feet and the socks. Dry skin is more resistant to blister formation than skin that has been softened by moisture. Beware powders that cake up and cause blisters. Good powders will absorb many times their weight in moisture.

The Second Line of Blister Defense

The second line of defense includes a variety of options. Skin tougheners, taping, orthotics, nutrition for the feet, proper hydration, anti-perspirants for the feet, gaiters, laces, and frequent sock and shoe changes each contributes to the prevention of blisters. Some of these options may be more important for your feet than for mine.

- Skin tougheners work three ways. They coat the feet for protection, toughen the skin, and, if you're using tape, help the tape or blister patches adhere better to the skin.

- Taping provides a barrier between the skin and your socks to reduce friction.

- Orthotics help maintain the foot in a functionally neutral position so arch and pressure problems are relieved. Small pads for the feet may also help correct foot imbalances and pressure points. Reducing these pressure points will help in reducing blisters.

- The use of creams and lotions on dry and callused feet helps soften the skin and make it resistant to blisters. The skin needs nutrients, particularly in the heat of summer and the cold of winter.

- Maintaining proper hydration helps reduce swelling of the feet, often common after hours of running, so the occurrence of hot spots and blisters is reduced. When you become fluid-deficient, the skin loses its normal levels of water and easily rubs or folds over on itself, leading to blisters.

• Those with extra sweaty feet may find the use of anti-perspirants helpful in reducing moisture on the feet that makes them more prone to blisters.

• Any trail runner should wear gaiters to provide protection against dirt, rocks, and grit. These irritants cause friction and blisters as shoes and socks become dirty.

• Adjusting shoelaces can relieve friction and pressure over the instep and make footwear more comfortable. Several alternatives to shoelaces are commonly found in running stores.

• For those completing extra-long runs or ultramarathons, frequent sock changes help keep the feet in good condition. Wet or moist shoes and socks can cause problems because the skin softens, maceration occurs, and skin layers separate. Changing socks also gives you the opportunity to reapply either powder or lubricant and deal with any hot spots before they become blisters.

Proactive or Reactive

You have the option of being proactive or reactive in managing blisters. The proactive runner takes steps to prevent blisters before they develop. The reactive runner treats the blisters after they develop. Many reactive runners simply think blisters are a normal part of running. Wrong! Working with the blister prevention options above can help eliminate one of the most troublesome problems in running.

John Vonhof is the author of Fixing Your Feet *and the proprietor of the highly informative website FixingYourFeet.com.*

When, despite your great care, you develop a hot spot on your foot, realize that this is the precursor to a blister. Some ultrarunners will knowingly ignore the hot spot and its possible consequences. This might be a reasonable course of action in a marathon or shorter race. However, when left untreated during an ultra, the hot spot has much more time to grow into a blister that will stop you dead in your tracks. That's why many ultrarunners who prefer to avoid prohibitively large blisters will attempt to resolve the cause of a hot spot at the next opportunity. The solution may be as simple as removing debris or adjusting either a sock or shoe. If no physical irritant is present, then it's time to apply tape or a blister pad, which will reduce the friction between the skin and sock or shoe that can cause a blister if left untreated.

If a blister forms, decide whether or not to treat it. Small or non-weight-bearing blisters can be treated with tape, moleskin, or blister pads. Large blood-free weight-bearing blisters may need to be drained and protected before continuing. If skin covering a blister is significantly torn, the skin should be cut away and antibiotic ointment should be applied before a protective covering is applied. Details for treating each type of blister are outlined in *Fixing Your Feet*.

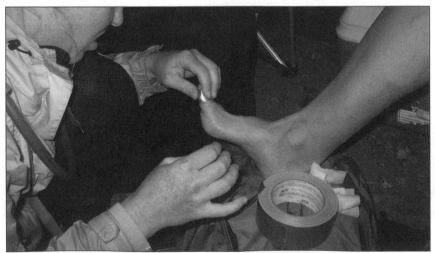

Proper attention prevents your feet from turning into a disaster.
(Photo courtesy of Alison Hanks)

If you routinely experience blistering during long runs, consider pre-taping the areas of your feet that give you the most problems. Pre-taping techniques arc also outlined in Mr. Vonhof's book.

Hang around ultrarunners long enough and you're bound to hear about black toenails. No, these runners aren't necessarily into nail polish. Rather, they've experienced blood or other fluid pooling under one or more of their toenails, technically known as subungal hematoma. Black toenails can be caused by acute trauma such as kicking a rock or by the toenail repeatedly hitting the front of the shoe, especially during downhills. If the toenail pain becomes unbearable, you can lance it to relieve the pressure. When the discoloration or pooled fluid extends to the tip of the toe, you can lance the pool by inserting a sterilized needle through the skin in front of the nail. When the fluid doesn't extend to the front of the toenail, you'll have to gently lance the pool through the toenail itself. Be sure to sterilize any lancing tools, to apply antibiotic ointment to the opening, and to monitor the affected toe in the days that follow. It is normal for the toenail to fall off in the months that follow.

Rhabdomyolysis and Kidney Failure

It should come as no surprise that severe muscle breakdown is common in ultramarathons. When skeletal muscle breaks down, it releases the protein myoglobin and other muscle components into the bloodstream. When severe, this muscle breakdown, known as rhabdomyolysis (rhabdo), can be harmful to the kidneys and, rarely, lead to acute kidney failure as the kidneys become clogged with myoglobin. I will stress that kidney-damaging rhabdo is rare; however, ultrarunners must be aware of the condition, its causes, its warning signs, and how to avoid it.

Rhabdo is most frequently seen in hot, mountainous, 100-mile races. There are good reasons for this. Rhabdo-inducing muscle breakdown is enhanced by eccentric muscle contractions. Eccentric muscle contractions occur when running downhill. Damage caused during eccentric muscle contractions is exacerbated by running down technical terrain and steeper descents as well as when descending when your running form has broken down due to fatigue. Obviously, the farther you run, the more opportunity there is for muscle breakdown to occur. In addition, the dangers of rhabdo are greatly increased by dehydration, which frequently occurs during ultras, particularly in hot weather. While it's common for urine to transition from clear to yellow during an ultra, precautionary steps for rhabdo should be taken when urine becomes cola-colored.

If you're a pacer, crew, or aid station volunteer and you suspect that a runner in your care has rhabdo, err on the side of caution in seeking medical attention. That often comes in the form of medical staff at the race.

Initial treatment of possible rhabdo is the same as for dehydration. That means oral rehydration with an electrolyte beverage or intravenous saline solution, depending on severity and availability. Finishing a race and heading right off to bed to recover is one of the worst things you could do. Rhabdo and associated kidney risks persist after the run is complete. Sleeping deprives you of the chance to rehydrate, while your kidneys remain subject to clogging. You're in the clear once you can urinate well with the urine color returning to normal shades. On the other hand, if flu-like symptoms develop, seek medical attention.

In extreme cases, hospitalization and hemodialysis will be necessary to prevent further kidney damage. On the upside, numerous ultrarunners who have been hospitalized for rhabdo have returned to top-level competition.

I Said, NSAIDs!

Ibuprofen, acetaminophen (Tylenol), and aspirin are among the most commonly used non-steroidal anti-inflammatory drugs (NSAIDs). Some ultrarunners take so much ibuprofen that they joking call it "Vitamin I." General prophylactic use of NSAIDs before workouts lessens the benefits of those workouts by limiting the body's natural healing response to inflammation. That healing response is what leads to stronger muscles, tendons, and bone. Properly dosed NSAIDs can be part of the effective treatment of an acute injury; however, be careful not to mask pain to the point where you are able to run in a manner that worsens the injury.

Excessive use of any NSAID—in particular, ibuprofen—can be dangerous. Much has been written warning about combining strenuous running (more than your daily run) and ibuprofen. It has been implicated in severe kidney problems among a few ultrarunners who took ibuprofen while dehydrated during a race.

I like to think I take a commonsense approach to NSAIDs in races. I don't take more than the recommended dosage at any time, I don't take more than two doses during a race, and I don't take NSAIDs if I am severely dehydrated. While I will take ibuprofen if it's the only option, I prefer to take Excedrin, which combines acetaminophen, aspirin, and caffeine. I hold off on using NSAIDs until the second half of a race. If there's a particularly nasty descent late in the race, I'll often take a dose 30 to 60 minutes before I begin it. Please note, I am not a medical professional and this is not medical advice. I am merely sharing my own choice. Make your own calculated, educated choices regarding NSAIDs and ultras.

[Author's Note: "The Lean" described below is a non-serious, non-permanent listing of a runner toward one side from the waist. The lean becomes more common as the length of an ultra increases and is most commonly seen in older men.]

The Lean

Scotty Mills

For those who have been around some of the longer ultras over the years, a not-so-common but very apparent race day condition known affectionately as "The Lean" can adversely affect ultra runners especially in the later stages of an event. There hasn't been a great deal written about this ailment, and it doesn't seem to be a chronic condition among most ultra runners. However, it can take a huge toll on a runner's body with regards to form, posture, and ability to continue moving to the finish line. The following observations and recommendations are simply from my personal perspective, as I have occasionally heard aid station volunteers and crew helpers say, "We have a leaner coming in!" Unfortunately, that leaner has been me on two separate occasions, at Western States and at the Wasatch 100.

I have done limited research and failed to identify this condition in any sports medical literature or scientific articles. I can only surmise that not much is written about runners' leaning because it occurs so infrequently and usually only at the very end of a long and grueling endurance event. Most would think that a weak back or unconditioned back muscles might be the root cause of this loss of control, but I am not convinced this is the case. Rather, my assertion is that the body is reacting to total exhaustion from the result of too many miles and hours of running on very challenging terrain and in hot daytime conditions.

This exhaustion may cause the body of the runner to lose some muscle control and balance.

My assumption in this regard is the fact that I work very diligently throughout my training to strengthen my core and back muscles. I have never had a back injury, and following a leaning episode I have no back or side pain the following day. I do know that the leaning episodes have occurred late in the event and at a time when I felt totally devoid of energy near or akin to "bonking," yet instead of feeling totally out of energy, the body seems to lose balance. So what to do to try to avoid The Lean?

As with bonking, I feel the most important thing an ultra athlete needs to do to avoid a "leaning condition" is to stay on top of hydration and energy replenishment from the very beginning of the race to the bitter end. This is obviously important for many other conditions that can adversely affect ultra runners, so The Lean is just another reason to work very diligently in training and race day to avoid energy depletion and exhaustion. If at any time in an ultra you feel yourself starting to lose balance and leaning is becoming a concern, my recommendation would be to slow down and force yourself to take on as much fluid and glycogen replacement as your stomach can handle. The thing you should not try to do is to keep going without addressing energy needs, as The Lean will progressively worsen and may result in an inability to stay upright on the trail. Another reason to avoid The Lean: Your finish line finish photo will not be your proudest of prizes.

Scott "Scotty" Mills has earned 15 silver buckles by running all 15 of his Western States 100s in less than 24 hours, despite finishing with a bout of leaning in 2006. As a race director and prominent member of the ultrarunning community, he's been an ultrarunning mentor to many, including the author of this book.

11

GEAR UP

Ultrarunning requires more gear than other running events. This chapter will familiarize you with gear options for running on trails, running in the dark, carrying your food, water, and other supplies, as well as navigating treacherous terrain.

Treat Your Feet Right

The one piece of equipment that nearly everyone uses during an ultramarathon is shoes. Everyone's feet and running gait differ, so generalized advice on shoe choice is hard to offer. Therefore, the best advice is to experiment and find what works for you. To the best of your ability, test your chosen model of race shoes on terrain and in conditions similar to those of race day, preferably during a long run. Even if you've worn the same model of shoes for a decade, log at least a few runs in your race day pair ahead of time to make sure the footbed position feels good and there are no unusual chafing points.

One thing to keep in mind is that feet often swell during ultras, particularly those beyond 50 miles. So, while it's important to find a shoe that fits securely to minimize blistering, it's also important that your shoe can accommodate a swollen foot. To test your shoes, run in your race shoes with a thicker-than-usual pair of socks to simulate swollen feet. A toebox that is roomier than normal also gives your foot room to expand.

If you'll be racing a trail ultra, decide whether to wear road or trail shoes. Know this: You don't need a trail shoe to run on trails. There is absolutely no reason a road shoe cannot be worn off-road.

In fact, many trail runners wear road shoes while competing in events as grueling as the Western States 100-mile run. That said, when you run off-road, trail shoes offer three primary advantages over road shoes: stability, traction, and protection.

Benefits of Trail Shoes

Stability

The rocks, roots, and uneven surfaces encountered on trail runs require more stability than runs on pavement. While road shoes are available in "stability" models, trail shoes provide a different sort of stability. Like road shoes, trail shoes can deliver stability via heel counters, supportive uppers, and variable-density midsoles; however, trail shoes have a few more tricks for the trail.

For instance, trail shoes tend to have thinner, denser midsoles for a lower-to-the-ground feel. This reduces the chance of turning an ankle and provides better responsiveness. The occasional trail shoe also throws in an outrigger flap on the rear or outside of the shoe that creates a wider platform for additional stability.

Traction

Road shoes achieve most of their traction through a large contact area with the ground. A flat outsole pattern also works well for trail shoes when worn on slickrock like that in Moab, Utah. Rock grip is enhanced when the outsole's rubber is softened, which makes it "sticky" like a climbing shoe.

Muddy or dusty trails require a completely different approach. If a trail's surface is likely to shift, then deep, aggressive lugs keep a runner from skidding out of control when stopping or turning. Aggressive outsoles tend to be heavier, so remember: Burlier isn't always better.

Protection

The same roots and rocks that warrant more stability in a trail shoe also call for more protection. Typical trail shoes include a thin rock plate that provides push-through protection from rocks and other debris. Trail shoe manufacturers have developed various rock plate patterns—ranging from rock plates that mirror the bones in your forefoot to ones that resembles trail switchbacks—that don't significantly interfere with a shoe's flexibility.

A trail shoe offers more than underfoot protection. Toe bumpers have turned countless would-be broken toes into mere awkward stumbles. While less frequently encountered, jutting rocks and roots can also tear at the instep and outside of the foot, which is where protective overlays work their magic.

Some trail shoes also feature a gusseted tongue or "scree guard" that prevents small debris from entering the shoe from around the tongue. Other shoes provide attachment points for gaiters—small fabric skirts that surround shoe uppers and extend over the ankle to prevent debris from entering through the ankle collar. These simple additions can be invaluable for preventing blisters that result from the increased friction of debris inside a shoe.

Adapted from the article "Do I Really Need a Trail Shoe?," which originally appeared on Running.Competitor.com.

When a run lasts many hours, wet feet can be debilitating. Trying to skirt every puddle and rock-hop across every stream is both frustrating and dangerous. In a steady rain, it's impossible to keep your feet dry, as shoes with waterproof membranes simply fill with water over time, turning them into fish bowls. Membrane shoes do, however, help your feet stay dry longer in light precipitation, when there's snow or slush on the ground, or when a storm is over, leaving only puddles. On the other hand, if stream crossings during your run infrequently but completely wet your feet in an otherwise relatively dry environment, opt for shoes that drain well and dry fast.

Open-mesh shoes are great for letting your feet breathe on a warm day. That same mesh also lets in dust and debris, though, a particular problem in arid environments. Therefore, a dusty or sandy course warrants choosing a shoe that lacks open mesh in favor of tighter mesh or fabric. A gusseted tongue, where a flap of fabric connects both sides of the tongue with the remainder of the shoe's upper, can help keep pebbles, twigs, and leaves from entering the front of your shoe. If you're worried about debris entering the top of your shoe, you can wear a low-cut, breathable gaiter made specifically for running.

Of course, there's the option of wearing little or no shoe. In recent years, barefoot running and minimalism have taken the running world by storm. Ultrarunning is no different. If you look around at an ultra, you'll see numerous runners in minimalist shoes akin to road racing shoes and a few runners wearing barely there shoes, if any at all. I'm not going to tell you which shoes you should or shouldn't wear. However, as with the rest of this chapter, I want to make you aware of the barefoot and minimalist running options. Even more so, I want to encourage those considering or involved in barefoot or minimalist running to do so thoughtfully and with restraint. I am not an expert on barefoot or minimalist running,* but Michael Sandler and Jessica Lee, publishers of RunBare.com and co-authors of *Barefoot Running*, are. In the appendix, Sandler and Lee outline the benefits of barefoot running, how to safely transition to it, and when it is appropriate to wear certain shoes.

---

* I do incorporate less structured, low heel-to-toe angle "minimalist"-style shoes into my running. During warmer months I may log up to four of my shorter runs each week in them to strengthen, stretch, and rehabilitate my lower legs and feet. After much research, I've made the personal decision to incorporate such shoes in my running gradually. With a history of Achilles tendonitis and plantar fasciitis, as well as many years of running in high-heeled running shoes, I feel that the benefits of a more dramatic shift to minimalist or barefoot running would not outweigh the significant risks.

Choosing a Shoe for the Trail

When you're hitting the trails, match the shoe to the conditions at hand. Although you can sport any old shoe to hit the trail, wearing the right shoe makes for a much more enjoyable experience. Below are some general categories of shoes that work best for different trail conditions.

The Roadie

Road shoes are a fine option on some trails, though they perform best on surfaces that resemble road. By all means, lace up your road shoes for trail runs with minimal hazards such as a crushed-stone bike path or a wood-chip trail. Do leave them at home when mud-bogging or imitating a mountain goat on rocky crags.

The Tank

If the rocks on your local trail are leaving your feet bruised and battered, it might be time to pick up a pair of tanks. While trail shoes are trending away from light hikers, there are days when you'll be thankful to have a wider platform, a thick rock plate, a big toe bumper, and a protective upper. Note, however, that these stiffer shoes rarely have as smooth a running feel as road shoes.

The Generalist

Generalist trail shoes are the bread and butter of dedicated trail companies. Designed for everyday trail runs starting at the trailhead, the generalist features a decent rock plate, a moderate lug pattern, and enough upper protection to keep you running the trails day after day.

The Hybrid

The hybrid trail–road shoe is where it's at for the many runners who need to hit the pavement for a few miles before reaching sweet singletrack. These shoes run like road shoes, but include lightweight versions of the protective features found in other trail shoes. A hybrid shoe is a great choice for any non-technical, off-road surface. Both road-shoe- and trail-shoe-focused companies are making quality hybrids these days.

The Claw and the Wing

Two specialty trail shoes, one for muddy trails and one for maximum speed, are more closely related than they look. Shoes for both conditions often have uppers stripped to the essentials. For the claw, this is to limit weight when wet, while the wing aims for the lightest possible weight all the time. Both shoes are likely to have a minimal rock plate for weight savings. The primary difference is that the claw comes with an über-aggressive tread pattern while the wing may hardly have any tread at all.

Adapted from the article "Do I Really Need a Trail Shoe?," which originally appeared on Running.Competitor.com.

Light Up the Night

Whether starting before daybreak or continuing past sundown, many ultras require running in the dark. If that night running is on a trail, you'll most likely want to carry a light source or two with you.

Headlamps are the most common light source seen at ultras. Any outdoor retail store has a selection of reasonably priced, approximately 3-ounce headlamps that provide more than adequate light for trail running at night. While there are larger, extremely bright headlamps, more modest headlamps are sufficient for most runners. Choose a headlamp that is rated to last more than an entire night without replacing the batteries.

Carrying a small, powerful, handheld flashlight is nearly as popular as wearing a headlamp. Some runners feel that the lower angle

A good light keeps you running safely all night.
(Photo by PatitucciPhoto.com)

of a flashlight provides them with better depth perception that aids in spotting rocks, roots, and other obstacles. The primary disadvantage of a flashlight is that it limits the use of one hand for other purposes. That means no trekking poles, only one handheld water bottle, and more difficulty with routine tasks such as opening a sports gel or taking an electrolyte tablet.

Although relatively uncommon, ultrarunners sometimes put a headlamp around their waist or use a pack with a light attached at the waist or sternum. These lights provide the same depth-perception benefits of a flashlight while freeing up your hands. However, when they're used without a second light source, it can be hard to spotlight a trail blaze or something that goes bump in the night.

Runners frequently combine two light sources to get the best aspects of each lighting system in addition to shedding more light on the trail. For instance, a headlamp–flashlight combination is quite popular. In this combination, the headlamp serves as a broad floodlight while the flashlight is used for spotting and depth perception. The combination also allows the runner to tuck the flashlight away temporarily if both hands are needed.

Whatever lighting option you employ, it's hard to go wrong with lighting sources based on light-emitting diodes or LEDs. Not so long ago, an ultrarunner had to carry a spare bulb in case his or her light burned out or broke. In the context of running, LEDs are nearly indestructible and have largely eliminated the need to carry backup lighting options. LED-based lighting systems do, however, have two quirks of which you should be aware. First, LED lights that lack a "regulator" quickly lose their maximum brightness before continuing to operate with slowly decreasing brightness for a long period. Regulated LEDs have the opposite problem. They maintain near-maximal output until the batteries are close to failure. For both these reasons, it's highly recommended that you change the batteries in any LED lights before a race even if the current batteries seem to be providing adequate light.

Getting Carried Away: Options for Hauling Gear

Ultra training and racing often warrant or mandate carrying food, fluids, and gear. When your hauling needs outmatch the storage capacity of your hands and pockets, it's time to pick up something with a bit more carrying capacity. Your options include waist packs and a variety of shoulder packs.

Waist or fanny packs are great for runs up to couple of hours as well as many races. Most waist packs hold a few essentials like keys, a few hundred calories of food, and some toilet paper. Adding an accessory pocket or two to the front of the waist strap expands the capacity of many packs. As mentioned in chapter 8, some waist packs include a rear holster or two for water bottles. You may need to experiment with a few models of water bottle waist packs to find one that neither bounces excessively nor ejects bottles during descents.

A small shoulder pack—with a capacity of 5 liters or less—is great for unsupported runs of half a day or more in good weather. These packs are also a reasonable racing option for those who don't like to wear something around their waists. A small shoulder pack lets you carry more water (up to 100 ounces) and more food (1,000-plus calories) as well as spare clothing, lighting, maps, and a few accessories. The front pockets on some models are great for accessing food or electrolyte tablets without stopping. Small capacity vest-style packs are increasingly popular, especially when racing, in large part due to their snug designs that minimize bouncing, even at faster paces. The primary drawback with vest-style packs is that they can be quite warm on hot days.

Except for races with long mandatory gear lists, you're unlikely to race with a shoulder pack that's 10 liters or larger. There are, however, many packs from 10 to 33 liters that are designed for running. Packs at the smaller end of this range are excellent for self-supported day-length runs and run commutes to and from work. Packs holding 20 or more liters are best suited for multiday adventures and races. Some multiday packs are available in multiple sizes for different torso lengths, so get fitted for the correct size.

Get Me Outta Here: Navigation on the Trail

Long training runs and, possibly, a sense of adventure get you out on the trails for some exploring. If you're lucky, you already know the local trail networks like the back of your hand or can find training partners who do. If not, you're on your own in finding your way around and out of unfamiliar territory and that requires carrying a map as well as some combination of a compass, GPS, and a good head on your shoulders. Always remember that you are ultimately responsible for your well-being on the trails.

Although cross-country navigation by way of map and compass has become a rarely practiced art, it remains essential to carry a trail map and know how to use it whenever you're exploring. Topographic

Plan your route ahead of time, but still bring your trail map with you!
(Photo by author)

maps, which display elevation contour lines as well as natural and man-made features, are the gold standard for trail maps. US Geological Survey (USGS) topographic maps, while infrequently updated, cover the contiguous United States and are widely available. The USGS, National Geographic Maps, and others offer printable digital maps with ever-increasing features, such as pre-digitized trails that allow you to quickly consider the distance and elevation profiles of various routes. Resources on how to read and navigate with a topographic map are available at :www.iRunFar.com/rfp/resources.

Once a novelty, the accuracy, feature set, and in some cases battery life of wrist-top GPS (global positioning system) units have improved greatly in recent years. Wrist-top GPS units often provide distance traveled, elevation, and compass bearing, each of which is useful to know for navigating with a topographic map. Some units also provide a "back to start" function that will help you backtrack should you find yourself unable to determine a route back to the trailhead. However, do keep in mind the fallibility of electronics (and their finite battery lives). While GPS devices are an excellent convenience, always be prepared to navigate the entirety of your route without their aid.

While not for all runners, the heart-rate option for many GPS units can be a helpful tool in both training and racing.

GPS Accuracy Tips

While GPS units have improved a great deal, a few simple steps can further increase their accuracy. Here are some tips to help you get the most out of your GPS:

1. Make sure the unit has the latest software for both the unit and the GPS chip set.

2. Before setting out on your run, leave the unit in clear view of the sky for two or three minutes. Sometimes you can reorient the device to pick up additional satellites that you wouldn't have acquired had you simply laid out the device. If you can view a graphic representation of locked and unlocked satellites on your unit, use this screen to assist in picking up additional signals by orienting the unit's antenna in the direction of the most non-locked satellites (unless there's a huge obstacle blocking that direction). Be aware that even with a clear "view" of a satellite signal, it can take the better part of an uninterrupted minute to obtain a lock, so be patient. Even though a GPS unit determines your position based on four satellites, locking additional satellites improves accuracy and reduces the chances of losing your GPS signal under trees or among sky-obscuring terrain.

3. Check on the GPS satellite status during the run. If possible, pick up new satellite locks en route. It's most useful to do this especially after passing through forested areas or canyons, or when a particular peak has obstructed a large portion of the sky for a while, such as when traversing the side of a steep mountain. Do this by consistently holding the unit's antenna toward the sky while moving . . . or repeating tip 2. The latter is easier and, if you still have some satellite locks, takes less time.

4. While it won't make your GPS more accurate, you can sometimes force a GPS unit to take measurements more often. However, the default recording rate is generally plenty accurate with more frequent recording options best kept for unusual uses, such as a race director measuring a course.

5. There are also training software and websites to which you can upload your GPS data and have the elevation profile or mileage accuracy enhanced.

12

RACING ULTRAMARATHONS

After many months of training, it's time for the big day: the day you race an ultramarathon. As with your training, there are numerous logistical and mental preparations to make prior to the race. On race day itself, you balance many competing needs. The unfamiliar environment and situations faced during your first few ultras makes balancing these needs a challenge.

This chapter informs you about the race-related choices and situations you'll face prior to and on race day. To start, you need to choose an ultra, so there's some advice for first-timers. Once you've chosen your event, set goals and expectations. You also have a good deal of pre-race preparation, including planning travel, researching and planning for the race's specifics, possibly choosing a support crew and pacer(s), and setting up drop bags. Then there's race day itself, so the chapter wraps up with general pacing advice, some insight into mental approaches, and a discussion of how to deal with injuries and aid stations.

Choosing Your First Ultra

I am often asked, "What's a good first ultra?" or the equivalent question for a particular distance. My answer? Nearly any ultra is a great first ultra or a first attempt at a longer distance. Each race has its own set of advantages. For example, a flat road course more closely resembles the races with which many runners are most familiar. On the other hand, a mountainous ultra provides built-in walking breaks, and the scenery offers a boost.

You could consider many factors in choosing a first ultra. However, if I suggest one as most useful, it is familiarity. This familiarity is either preexisting or learned. If you live where there are mountain trails out your back door and there's a race on those trails, run it! Even if the nearest ultras are an hour or two from where you live, consider running one of those races. You don't need to run the race course every day to know it well. Rather, consider making the course the site of some of your long training runs.

If you don't live near or can't easily get to any ultra locations, consider talking to others who have run ultras. Find out as much as you can about a particular race. (This is a good idea even if you run some or all of the course before race day.) Even if you've run for years, it's great to know how to train best for a particular course and strategies for approaching the course on race day, such as where to be prepared for various conditions (heat, cold, water crossings, darkness) or how much water to carry between particular aid stations. Before my first 100-miler, the 2004 Western States 100, I attended a race briefing put on by three of my clubmates. Before I ever arrived at the start line, I felt like a race veteran. I knew the course and how to approach it.

Setting Goals and Expectations

Setting race goals is extremely motivating before and during a race. They get you out the door on a miserable morning months before your race or push you through fatigue in the final miles on race day. In order to set an effective goal, be honest with yourself. What are the true reasons you're running a particular ultra? There are likely to be many.

If this is your first ultra, simply finishing, no matter how ugly that finish may be, is a good place to start. Indeed, crossing the finish is often the primary goal even among veteran ultrarunners with particular time or placing goals in mind. Unlike a 5k or 10k, there is significant uncertainty that any runner will finish a given ultra.

Not everyone needs to "race" the ultra distance. If your goal is to have a new adventure, enjoy the trails, or have fun, stay true to that goal. Setting such a goal is still motivating in training, as improving your fitness makes it easier to finish the ultra without undue struggle.

Okay, so just finishing or having fun isn't for everyone. Many among us enjoy having time or place goals. Sometimes these time goals arise naturally, such as when there's a qualifying standard for a future race, there's a round number to shoot for (say, 10 or 12 hours for a 50-miler or 24 hours for a 100), or there's a race cutoff that's a serious consideration. Just as often, ultrarunners set more abstract time or place goals.

Before you run your first ultra, setting realistic time or place expectations is exceedingly difficult. Extrapolating road marathon times to a trail ultra is dodgy at best. Your best bet is to ask the opinion of veteran ultrarunners with whom you have run and who have run or are at least very familiar with the race in question. If that's not an option, look at the recent years' results for the race you're debuting at and see if any names are familiar. Perhaps there are some runners whom you previously finished close to at other races. The shorter the races in common, the less reliable any comparison is, but you gain a ballpark sense of time. Honestly, it's often best to avoid setting an arbitrary time goal in your first ultra. Run based on effort and be happy with your finishing time, whatever it is.

Once you have one or more ultras under your belt, it's much easier to come up with time goals to shoot for. While you're new to the sport, talking with veterans is still a good idea. Start cross-referencing your prior ultras with the race for which you're building a time goal. To do so, identify a runner whom you've finished near in a prior ultra who has also finished your target race. This runner's time in a prior version of your target race gives you a sense of where you could finish. Finding additional runners with whom to form comparisons builds a more accurate prediction, as one runner's relative performance varies quite widely between any two races.

If you've already raced the same distance as the race you're contemplating, take a broad look at the times for these races, particularly around the percentile in which you've previously finished. This gives you a sense for whether the upcoming course is faster or slower than those you've previously raced; if you compare the results closely enough, you might even get a sense of by how many minutes the new course is faster or slower.

Pre-Race Preparations

Logistical decisions made months ahead of race day play a significant role in ultramarathon success. Among these decisions are travel; choosing a support crew and pacers, if desired; determining everything that is needed before, during, and after the race (and packing it!); and preparing drop bags.

Travel Plans

For many, the choice between driving and flying to a race is determined largely by travel distance, time constraints, and cost. That said, travel and its effects are highly personal. Over the years, you've likely learned the degree to which flying across the country or driving a long distance wears you out. Take this into consideration when planning travel to your ultramarathons. If you'll travel for more than six or eight hours, aim to arrive at your destination no later than early to midafternoon the day before the race. This gives you time to rehydrate, stretch out, make final preparations, eat a decent meal, and decompress while still getting some sleep. As will be explained in chapter 13, arrive as early as possible when you're traveling from low altitude for a high-altitude race.

Along with your own travel plans, you may be making travel plans for others. Unlike marathon and shorter races, it's common for two sets of people, a support crew and a pacer or pacers, to assist a runner during an ultra.

Race Research and Planning

One of the most exciting aspects of ultras is the extreme variety found in the different races. This doesn't apply just to the courses, but to the rules as well. Carefully research both prior to race day.

As described in chapter 3, specificity is an important part of training. When you start training, look at the race's elevation profile to determine how hilly it is and research what the footing is like. Train accordingly. In addition, determine if the race is subject to extreme heat, cold, or altitude and whether it's likely you'll be running in the dark. How to approach each of these challenges is outlined in chapter 13.

Early in your race planning process, research whether the race allows support crews and pacers—two forms of personal, in-race support—and whether you want either or both to be part of your ultramarathon experience.

In the weeks ahead of the race, look at the distance and topography between aid stations and roughly estimate how long you think it will take you to get between each of them. Based on those time estimates and broad temperature guesses based on time of day, figure out how much fluid you'll need between aid stations. This informs your choice of hydration carrying methods, discussed in chapter 8.

At the same time, start planning what gear and nutritional supplies you ideally want to pick up or drop off at each aid station. This means picking up a resupply of gels, a headlamp, a change of socks and shoes, or a fresh shirt, among many other things. It also means getting rid of gear you no longer need, but don't wish to part with forever. Now see if the race transports drop bags. Discussed more fully later in this section, drop bags are a way to get some of your supplies to designated aid stations. Then start planning what you want to pick up or drop off at particular aid stations based on where you can have a crew or a drop bag.

As a race nears, I develop both a checklist and a to-do list. The checklist is a list of all the items I need for the trip and the race. Sit down and write an initial checklist, but allow it to grow over time as you think of new items. I include everything down to my wallet and phone. Once you draft a pre-race checklist, save it and modify it for future races. I feel much more assured in packing if I have a checklist to follow. Just remember not to cross an item off the checklist until you put it in your bag, suitcase, pocket, or car. My to-do list covers pre-travel items, but focuses on what I need to do the day or two prior to a race and before the start on race day. The list assures that I won't forget an important pre-race step. It also encourages me to plan out a reasonable schedule for the hours prior to the race by moving as many items as possible from race day to an earlier day.

Sample: My To-Do List for the 2009 Leadville 100

Thursday
- Shake-out run
- Look at gel selection

Friday
- Grocery and last-minute supply shopping
- Charge GPS unit
- Pack post-race bag
- Empty cooler
- Empty unnecessary stuff from car
- Pack gear
- Shower and shave before bed

Race Morning
- Pack iPod Shuffle and preferred headphones
- Hydrate
- Apply sunblock
- Apply Bodyglide to inner thighs
- Apply nipple Band-Aids

Support Crews

Many ultras allow a runner to have a support crew, a person or people that assist at designated aid stations along the course.* While a crew can provide useful psychological support, its primary duties are usually logistical. This might mean that your crew brings your desired food, drink, and gear to specific aid stations while you take care of your own needs. Or you could have your crew take a much more active role in asking you questions, assessing your state, assisting with shoe and clothing changes, filling water bottles or a hydration bladder, and taking care of any other needs you have.

Some ultrarunners, myself included, envision their crew as a Formula 1 car racing crew with a plan designed to minimize time in an aid station. For example, when I enter an aid station, I drop my empty bottles; my crew asks me short, predetermined questions; they hand me full bottles and additional fuel; and we exchange additional gear, such as a headlamp as evening approaches, that I've scheduled for pickup or drop-off at that aid station. That's it. It may sound like a lot, but when it's done well I can walk straight through a crewed aid station without stopping. I'm not asked any questions about creature comforts or what I might "want." Additional issues are only addressed if I feel they are necessary. To save time, if an issue is not critical, I often let my crew know what I need and ask them to have it ready when I next see them.

Why am I sharing all this now rather than in the "In-Race Strategy" section that follows? Two reasons.

First, you need to assemble your crew and make sure that their travel and lodging arrangements are set, whether by you or them.

---

* I speak of crews and, in the next subsection, pacers with regard to their "duties." By providing these instructions, I merely aim to help an aspiring or novice ultrarunner make the best use of his or her crew or pacer. Having either is a gift. Be thankful for their assistance, whatever it may be, and their willingness to share your ultramarathon experience. Until you've filled each role yourself, you might underestimate how difficult the roles of crew and pacer are. Try both to learn more about the sport, to appreciate the difficulties associated with each role, and to help out your fellow runners.

For the most part, people ask their friends and family to crew, for obvious reasons. Generally, a crew consists of one or two people, but can be larger. If you're new to ultras, it's helpful but unnecessary to include a veteran ultramarathoner or ultra crew member in the ranks of your crew. He or she will know what to expect and can help direct any other crew members.

Second, you need to determine what exactly you'll have your crew do. What will they bring to aid stations? What will you expect them to do with it? Should they have certain items ready or be prepared to assist with preset tasks at specific aid stations? How would you prefer for them to interact with you on race day? It's important to be realistic about what you, personally, expect you'll want and need on race day. Everyone approaches races differently; you should assemble your crew and provide them with instructions that match your approach.

Before race day, be sure to give your crew adequate instructions. That might mean a simple five-minute chat. If you're unlucky enough to be on my crew, it means an eight-page single-spaced document supplemented by individual briefings. Previous crew members only wish I was kidding.

A supportive crew is often a welcome addition at an ultra.
(Photo courtesy of Bill McGovern)

Pacers

Some ultras, particularly races of 50 miles or longer, allow you to have a runner accompany you on later sections of the course. These runners are known as pacers. With few exceptions, the pacer's role is limited to mental support in that they are prohibited from carrying any of your gear. They can, however, give you a mental boost or break, help keep you on course, and act as your brain when yours is fried. They can also help assess your state and offer lucid suggestions for bettering it. When I'm pacing, I often tell a runner when he or she should eat, drink, take electrolyte tabs, and even when to run or walk. A good story, a raunchy joke, some encouraging words, a kick in the pants, or resounding silence all fall within a pacer's support role.

The term *pacer* is a misnomer at times, as some races require the racer to run in front of the pacer. However, at many ultras, the pacer can lead. The advantage of having a pacer lead is that he or she can scan for the best running line on a trail as well as keep an eye out for course markings. This allows you to concentrate more on your needs. While leading, a pacer can also subtly encourage a slightly faster pace.

As with a crew, find a pacer or pacers (each pacer would run a different section) who suit your needs. If you think you want someone to carry on a multihour monologue to entertain you, don't ask your friend Silent Bob to pace you. Likewise, try to find someone who matches your preferred motivation, be it Cheerleader Charlie or Drill Sergeant Dan. All that said, I've had amazingly good luck being paired with pacers whom I hadn't met until just before or, sometimes, when they joined me on course. It's refreshing to have someone share his or her life story for the first time while out on the trail. Some races provide runner-pacer-matching services. If that's not the case for a particular race, friends, social networks, and online forums are great places to look for potential pacers.

Perhaps even more so than with crew members, beginning ultrarunners benefit from having veteran ultrarunner pace them. That veteran ultrarunner commiserates (and you're more likely to believe him or her), assesses your needs, and suggests solutions.

Drop Bags

Many ultras allow another, more self-reliant form of racer support—the drop bag. Drop bags have nothing to do with dropping out of the race; rather, they are bags you fill with supplies that the race drops off at designated aid stations for you to access. Drop bags are extremely handy if you race without a crew. Without drop bags, you need to carry all of the materials you want, but are not available at aid stations, for the entire race. Even if that's only two dozen sports gels, a headlamp, and a change of shoes, it's awfully nice not to have to carry that weight. Even if you have a crew, drop bags are handy at aid stations where crews are not permitted or if you decide prior to the race that your crew won't go to an aid station where crews are permitted. Common items for drop bags are particular foods or drinks not provided by the race, a change of shoes and socks, as well as a headlamp and warm clothes for the night.

Drop bags hold your supplies that some races deliver to pre-designated aid stations. (Photo by Stephan/Gripmaster)

Do the race a favor and don't pile everything but the kitchen sink in your drop bags! Pack what you need, but no more.

If a race returns through the start area one or more times, you can often set up an unofficial drop bag there. I've never had a problem with a race official or theft when doing this.

In-Race Strategy

Nerves are completely natural before a race, particularly if you are moving up to a new distance. Use the advice in this section to take the right approach on race day. Go out slow, maintain an even effort, have the right mental approach, be proactive with your problem solving, have an aid station strategy, and, most important, have fun! How to do each of these is explained below.

Go Out Slow

The most useful piece of race day advice I can give a new ultramarathoner and many veteran ultramarathoners is to go out slower than you think you should. We've all been at marathons or shorter races where we're sucked into too fast a pace for the first portion. This is natural. We're excited and let it get the better of us. Well, the same thing happens all the time in ultras. In fact, it may be even more common in ultras as, unlike shorter races, the "too fast" pace isn't taxing in the early miles of an ultramarathon. It's easily maintained and, depending on the pace of daily training runs, may feel more comfortable than the pace we should try to maintain throughout the entire ultra. If you're ever breathing hard in ultra, it's time to consider whether you're running too fast!

To control my pace in the first half of an ultra, when I'm X miles from the start, I consider whether I'll be able maintain that same effort X miles from the finish. I acknowledge that I will inevitably be somewhat slower at a given effort later in the race; however, if there's a significant gap between the intensity I'm running and what I think I can run late in the race, I slow down. In most cases, trying

...these 3 guys are behind you and you're NOT Dave Mackey!

Remember to control your pace early in an ultra.
(Comic by EJ Murphy, creator of Ultra Running Guy comics)

to run 15 or 30 seconds faster per mile in the early going of an ultra is a fool's errand. Gaining five minutes in the first 10 miles can too easily cost half an hour or more later in the race, if not prevent you from finishing at all.

To run to your absolute potential, it's necessary to push the pace early on in the hope that everything goes right throughout the day. I don't think this risk is worthwhile for most runners, who will be able to run close to their potential with a more conservative strategy. If every last second is important to you, it's best to develop more aggressive race plans by dialing in your maximum sustainable effort for given lengths of time through experience. Accordingly, such attempts are not recommended for ultramarathon rookies.

Maintain an Even Effort

Next to starting conservatively, maintaining an even effort might be the most important race day ultra advice. In chapter 9, you learned that as you ramp up intensity, you increase the proportion of carbohydrates you burn in comparison with fat. Conserving your sugar supplies so that they are available throughout the race is vital. Should you run out of sugar to burn, you will bonk and be reduced to running or walking at an effort where you are tapping only your fat stores. This is both slow and unpleasant. Avoiding spikes in your heart rate goes a long way toward setting yourself up for success late in an ultra.

In most trail ultras, this means coming to terms with idea of walking at any point after the gun goes off. When you come to an incline or hill, decide if you should walk it. Practice making this determination during hilly, long training runs. This practice helps you roughly determine on what degree incline you can continue running with an even heart rate and which should be walked. Do not run up a hill until you are panting or can't run before deciding to walk. Walking while running trails is more fully discussed in chapter 7.

Mental Approaches to Race Day

Standing at the starting line, the thought of running an ultra can be overwhelming. There's no getting around the fact that 30 miles or more is long way to run. The best way to deal with this is not to think about the whole distance. Instead, break the run up into smaller sections. The most common way to do this is to run from aid station to aid station. As motivation later in the race, consider setting goals of running to the next tree or the boulder 100 yards down the trail.

On race day be prepared for a roller coaster of energy and emotions. While you'll hopefully avoid bonking completely, it's natural for energy to ebb and flow during an ultra. If it's ebbing, make sure that you're taking in enough calories. It's quite possible that you are and, if that's the case, you'll just need to ride it out. Try not to get frustrated with the situation. It's just something that happens in ultras.

Even if your energy levels remain high, your emotional state can plummet without warning. Such emotional downfalls can seemingly be triggered by minor or inconsequential events like stumbling, having difficulty opening or putting away an item, or frustration with the availability of items at an aid stations. They also come out of nowhere. If you find yourself unreasonably frustrated or down, you might not be able to reverse your mood quickly. However, knowing and reminding yourself that such dark spells are common parts of ultramarathons keeps you moving forward while you weather the storm.

Negative emotions aren't the only emotions amplified during ultras. Euphoric states aren't a given in any single ultra, but you're likely to experience them if you run enough of them. I fondly remember one while running along the American River (roughly miles 65 through 75) during the 2005 Western States 100. I was jubilant and amazed at what the human body is capable of. While I ran a great split during that section, I caution you to take advantage of such good times, but not to get so carried away that you pay the price later when the euphoric state passes.

Know, too, that it's common to be emotional. Crying for little or no reason as well as other strong upwelling of feeling happen late in ultras. Don't become overly concerned about these. They are part of the ultramarathon journey.

Race Day Problem Solving

Expect the unexpected on race day, as it will happen. Be willing to deviate from the plan you laid out. Part of the point of long training runs and tune-up races is to encounter the same problems you may face on race day. This allows you to learn how to recognize and successfully deal with an issue before it becomes a huge problem.

During a race, be vigilant in observing your body's own signs. It's easy to focus wholly on your race plan and making relentless forward progress. In fact, it's often much easier to zone out than to be in the moment. While you can zone out from time to time, you need to regularly check back in with yourself. When you sense something is not right, contemplate its significance. Take action to make it better sooner than later. Be proactive, not reactive. That's to say, recognize and remediate your problems before they derail your race.

Discomfort is almost a given in an ultramarathon. Learning to determine the difference between discomfort and injury is important. While I'm no doctor and this is not medical advice, dull aches and stiffness tend to be harmless discomfort. Continuing through discomfort is less likely to have long-lasting consequences. The decision to persevere is based on your own willingness to deal with the discomfort and the desire to continue. Stabbing or other acute pains, on the other hand, more likely indicate a serious injury that could have a lasting effect. If medical personnel are available on the course, seek their opinion as to whether continuing will likely lead to long-term or permanent injury.

While no one likes to drop out from a race, it's sometimes the prudent thing to do. To reduce the chances of serious regret, consider the issue of dropping out well ahead of race day. Decide under what conditions you are willing to drop out and what conditions are unacceptable reasons for dropping. This is especially important if you have a chronic injury. Determine the extent to which you are willing to push yourself through this injury should it act up on race day.

Across the Highland Sky:
A Story of In-Race Management

Eric Grossman

I'm running on the Road Across the Sky. I've got five Pringles in my left hand, and one in my right. I try to keep my lungs full, exhaling about half the volume with each breath. The painful tugging runs from my ribs to my belly just right of mid line. I know my ileo psaos is cramping. I push the single Pringle in my mouth and chew. It soaks up the little saliva in my mouth and turns into a dry chewy clump. I grab my bottle from my waist pack and fill my mouth with water so I can swallow. I'm able to get through three more chips this way. I pitch the last two.

Brian Schmidt runs alongside. We don't talk much. Not because it's a race, and we're battling at the front. We have emerged after more than 20 miles of steep, rocky, mountain single track. After miles of ankle-twisting, body-jarring scrambling up, down, and back up the lush mountain, I eagerly anticipated the chance to run out in the open. Now I feel overexposed as we run across the highlands. The road stretches out interminably in front of us. I welcome a companion through this inviting, yet inhospitable, place. Within our quiet is a shared focus—to maintain ourselves.

Very long runs will inevitably require attention to maintenance: to hydration, electrolytes, and fueling—and usually in that order. Running well for many hours requires successful management of these elements. Failure is felt as exhaustion, cramping, nausea, bloating, light-headedness, and other unpleasant sensations. Ultimately, failure to manage is felt as a complete loss of motivation to continue. It usually takes an ultramarathon to get to this point, though, because under normal conditions we have a couple hours buffer built in—the reserves stored in our bodies. Experienced ultrarunners carry water bottles, salt tablets, and high-energy snacks to supplement those stores. Of course, conditions aren't always normal.

Courses can be set that are challenging by design. Highland Sky is like that: a couple of fast road miles to lure you in, a huge climb to drain your stores, a precipitous descent to bash your quads, then more climbing to rock-strewn boulder fields that take all of what is left of your mental focus. And then, still less than halfway through, you are left to bake on a wide-open stretch of road across the top of the mountain.

That's where I am when I'm confronted with demons of races past. The painful abdominal cramps that caused me to drop from a race for the first time. The cotton mouth that I've experienced many times in warm weather races. The deadly potential of low blood-sodium that I experienced twice before I knew what it was. Even considering the difficult course, and the summer heat and humidity, I should not have been struggling after only three hours.

I slept little the night before, and got up with intestinal distress. Some of that is typical race stress—but this was disproportionate for me. I drank some of my homemade energy shake, a concoction of yogurt and blueberries that was untested as a pre-race meal. For the run, I packed several packs of Clif Bloks in my waistpack, along with my water bottle and salt tablets. I methodically emptied my water bottle between aid stations, and took an S-cap each hour, but the Clif Bloks went untouched for 20 miles. It was time to take stock.

I had benefited from the work of other runners up to that point. Sean Andrish led up the big climb, taking some of the sting out of the nettles, and setting a strong steady effort that contoured to the terrain. Sean's vast trail running experience was evident. Jeremy Ramsey has also paid some dues, and was able to take over pacing duties throughout the most technical sections of the run. He established himself as one of the three best rock runners I have run behind. Clark Zealand, who gapped me on through those same sections seven years ago, dances across rocks like a kind of forest spirit. Dave Mackey runs through rocks like a locomotive. Jeremy just picks the most economical line possible and scoots through it. To the extent I kept him in sight, my best strategy was to follow him. We all knew that a shake-up was likely. The Highland Sky course, perhaps more than any other, changes abruptly. We didn't just go from technical singletrack trail to open dirt road. We went from forest canopy to exposed meadow. We went from hazy shade to glaring light. And an aid station where my wife waited. She couldn't believe I hadn't eaten. I traded Clif Blok flavors around—it didn't matter though—I would only eat one pack the entire run.

I finally led the way down that first section of road. I choked down two Bloks. I backed off the intensity in response to the cramping and dry-mouth. At the next aid station I grabbed the short stack of Pringles. Small bites of savory snacks, interspersed with sips of water, help me keep it together. The race became a lesson in management. Small bites, small sips. Short strides uphill. Arms lightly swinging, hands loose. Recognize the despair; chalk it up to low blood sugar and dehydration. Manage it. Small bites, small sips. Flow across the ground.

I proceeded across and down the mountain in that way, resolutely clinging to the edge of what was possible. Technically, at every point of the race I could have tried harder. My sense, then and now, is that if I had tried harder, at any point of the race, things would have turned out worse. Had I resisted the truth of the situation, or imagined I had any special power to buoy myself above it, my flight would have melted like the wax of Icarus' wings. What I did have, and use, was the experience of countless prior moments. I do mean the sort of technical expertise to manage fluid and fuel consumption. More importantly, I mean the management of my motivation, or will, to carry on with what is ultimately a recreational activity.

Eric Grossman is an elite runner and college professor in Southwestern Virginia. Over the past decade and a half, he's run more than 50 ultras and won many of them, including the 2010 Highlands Sky 40 and 2009 Miwok 100k.

Aid Station Strategy

Aid stations are a wonderful thing. Without aid stations, you would have to carry all your own food, water, and supplies through the entirety of an ultra. Sure, this is quite possible and is done all the time on longer training runs, but it sure is nice to run a race with minimal encumbrance. Still, countless minutes or even hours can easily be frittered away in aid stations. Spending as little as two minutes in each aid station adds up to nearly an hour in the 29-aid-station Vermont 100!

Much of that time need not be wasted. To minimize aid station time, prepare your basic aid station plan prior to the race as described in the "Support Crew" and "Drop Bag" subsections earlier in this chapter. Whether or not you have a crew and drop bags at a race, you'll likely have to deal with aid stations without such luxuries, as few ultras have crew access or drop bag service at all aid stations. Thus, plan for these "self-service" aid stations as well.

Most aid stations are usually far from self-service. Indeed, the vast majority are staffed by volunteers who are eager to help you. Sometimes this assistance and the vast array of food, beverage, and creature comforts (chair and a wet towel, anyone?) is overwhelming. The best way to deal with the plethora of choices and minimize aid station time is to plan what you need at a given aid station before you get there. There's plenty of time on the trail to mull over the general choices—which beverages, what types of food, what issues need to be taken care of. If you have trouble remembering, develop a mnemonic or tell your pacer, if you have one.

Remember that one of your aid station options is to run right through the aid station without stopping. This option is best employed at races with aid stations that are close together.

Once you're in the aid station, attend only to the needs you determined while out on the trail. Don't be swayed by offers for things you don't need or stand dumbstruck by the bounty of food available. If volunteers are offering to fill your water bottle or hydration pack, let them. Just prior to the aid station, remove the tops of the bottles to be filled or make your hydration bladder accessible. Simultaneously, take care of your other aid station needs while the kind volunteer is refilling your hydration system.

A chair is a sight for sore legs in an aid station. Beware the chair! It's always harder to get up than you think it will be. Plus, every time you sit, there's a small but real chance that, physically or mentally, you won't be able to get back up. One reason to sit might be to change your shoes, if a pair is available from your crew or a drop bag. Aside from changing out of wet shoes when I know my new shoes will stay dry for a substantial period, I avoid changing my shoes unless I have foot problems very early in the race or I have severe foot pain. In my personal calculus, I would rather stick with a pair of shoes that has gradually led to moderate blistering or foot pain over many miles rather than risk changing into shoes that could be far worse.

Whether you change shoes or not, there's one last thing to do before leaving the aid station—thank the volunteers!

Have Fun!

There will be trying times in an ultra, but enjoy what you can of it. Take in the scenery. Talk with friends and strangers alike. Lose yourself in thought or zone out. Marvel at your accomplishment or laugh at your foolishness. Laugh. If it's a rainy mess, jump in some puddles. If it's hot, jump in a stream. Let out a triumphant cheer at the top of a climb and a joyous holler as you fly down a hill. Be a kid. Be happy.

13

ENVIRONMENTAL CONDITIONS*

Before I go scaring anyone, I need to reaffirm that most ultras, road or trail, are run in hospitable environments. Sure, they're long and difficult, but the conditions under which they're run are within the range of your normal running experience or within a mind's leap of it. And then there are a few ultras held under conditions that make the already difficult nearly unfathomable. There's the searing heat of the Badwater Ultramarathon and Marathon des Sables, the breath-stealing altitude of the Leadville and Hardrock 100-milers, and the bone-chilling cold of the Susitna 100-mile. This chapter looks at the effects of each of these conditions—heat, high altitude, and cold—and how to deal with them.

The Heat Is On

Hot weather is by far the most common extreme condition ultramarathoners experience. Sometimes ultrarunners face the smothering reality of "hazy, hot, and humid." Other times that heat presents itself as a moisture-sucking dry heat that feels like you opened an oven door in your face. While these types of heat have different effects, both present performance and health issues.

Performance and Acclimation

Whether we're looking to finish or to win the race, most of us go into an ultra with performance goals in mind. Heat can directly limit

---

* The information found in this chapter is not a substitute for medical diagnosis or treatment.

Stream and river crossings offer a welcome reprieve on a hot day.
(Photo by Glenn Tachiyama)

performance by diverting blood flow from muscles to the skin for cooling, and indirectly by causing dehydration, the performance-limiting effects of which were explained in chapter 8. I'll leave it to Dr. William Henderson to explain the effects of heat on running and how to acclimate in case you'll be racing in extreme heat.

Heat Performance and Acclimation

William Henderson, MD, FRCPC

There is little doubt that exercise performance is impaired in hot environments. While the effect of heat on performance varies with the sport (for example, it has less effect on cycling than running), there is a great deal of empirical data showing a link between ambient temperature and performance. Various authors have suggested performance impairments of 1.6 to 3 percent in marathon times for every 10 degrees above 55 degrees Fahrenheit. The effect seems to be less dramatic for faster runners.

How Heat Affects Running Performance

Why are we slower in hot conditions? There are a variety of proposed mechanisms, but the one that is most widely accepted is based on cardiac output limitations.

When we exercise, we produce a great deal of heat. One of the principal ways that we get rid of this excess heat is through sweating (evaporative heat loss), as well as conduction and radiation of heat from our skin. To achieve this, our bodies have to send a considerable amount of blood to the skin. This blood is therefore not available to perfuse working muscles and deliver oxygen to them. So a portion of our blood volume is essentially no longer able to participate in oxygen delivery and energy formation in our exercising muscles. The greater the amount of heat that we need to dissipate, the greater the proportion of blood that is diverted to the skin (up to a point—this can't increase forever).

What is necessary for cooling isn't the hemoglobin (the red blood cells in blood) but the plasma, which is essentially water with a number of different proteins and electrolytes in it. However, your body can't separate the red cells (which are the oxygen carriers) from the plasma—they all go along for the ride to the skin.

How We Acclimate to Heat

If it's plasma that is the essential cooling component, is it possible to improve this problem by increasing our total plasma volume? Yes, and that is exactly what happens as we adapt to heat over time. Whether you acclimate naturally to higher temperatures over the course of a season, or in a heat chamber, the most significant change that occurs is an increase in plasma volume. Other things occur as well (such as changes in sweat sodium concentration, resting core temperature, and heart rate), but plasma volume expansion is the key. After extensive acclimatization, plasma volume can have expanded by as much as 2 liters!

This may explain why the fittest athletes adapt to heat stress more quickly than the less fit. One of the by-products of endurance training (especially at high intensities) is an increase in plasma volume. So just by training hard, you can derive some amount of heat acclimation.

Aside from the increase in plasma volume, there are some other physiological adaptations that occur during heat training—changes in sweat rate, changes in sweat sodium concentration, and changes in core resting temperature, to name a few. The various adaptations occur with different amounts of acclimatization. Here's a graphical representation of the times over which an athlete can gain these benefits:

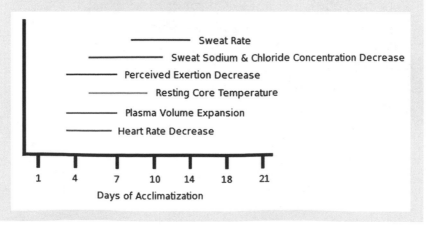

In my own low-intensity heat acclimation program for the 2009 Marathon des Sables,* my heart rate at the same speed and temperature decreased by about 9 percent—a very significant improvement—following just nine sessions. Now, it didn't get as low as what I would expect it to be in "normal temps," but the improvement was significant, and could be expected to translate into a tangible benefit in competition.

Heat Acclimation Methods and Considerations

The work needed to achieve the benefits of heat acclimation is reasonable. Most laboratory-based heat acclimation protocols have athletes spend about one hour a day in a heat chamber for 7 to 10 days. Importantly, this needs to occur as close to the time of the competition as possible, as the adaptations conferred by acclimation decay rapidly without ongoing exposure. So there's no point in spending two weeks in a heat chamber a month before the race without intervening heat exposure—the effects will decay in one to three weeks.

Estimates of heat acclimation decay vary, but it's possible that you could lose half of the benefit in 10 days without ongoing heat exposure. This raises some logistical problems for athletes living in cold environments who are attempting to acclimate for a hot-weather event. To benefit maximally from acclimatization, the heat training sessions should occur as close as possible to the event. That seems pretty straightforward. The problem is that acclimation is quite physically demanding, and most athletes attempt to taper in the week(s) prior to a big race. So if you want to acclimatize optimally, it needs to occur during your taper—which may cause overtraining, or at least minimize the benefits of tapering.

---

* During the acclimation program, I ran on a treadmill at 60 percent VO_2 max for 45 to 75 minutes for nine sessions. The first three sessions were at 95 degrees F (35 degrees C); the next five were at 113 degrees F (45 degrees C). The last (ninth) session occurred at 95 degrees F again—this allowed us to compare my physiological data from the first and the last sessions.

As with all training, the more specific, the better. When it comes to heat acclimatization, this means that your training climate should reflect the competition environment as closely as possible—the same temperatures as well as the same humidity. Why is humidity important? As anyone who has survived an East Coast summer knows, humidity makes it harder to lose heat via sweating. Training in a humid environment does confer some benefit if you are training for a dry, hot race, but not as much as training in a dry, hot chamber. Interestingly, there is better "transfer" of acclimation if you train in a dry, hot climate and then race in a humid, hot race than the other way around. So as much as possible, match humidity and temperature of your acclimation phase to your race environment.

What about passive acclimation? That is, will sitting in a sauna at the YMCA get us ready for running in Death Valley? Essentially—a bit, but not much. Acclimatization is vastly greater (and more rapid) if you exercise during the heat exposure. Whether this is again the principle of specificity, or whether it's simply that core temperature rises faster with active acclimation (increased core temperature is probably the stimulus for the adoptions that occur), is not clear.

Stay Hydrated!

One of the most important ways to prevent heat injuries and maintain performance in extremely hot environments is to drink adequate amounts of fluid. This seems obvious, but it is actually surprisingly hard to do this if you are focusing on running. I think that one of the most useful benefits (for me—not living somewhere hot) of heat acclimation sessions was learning to drink earlier and more frequently.

Conclusion

In my experience, heat acclimation based on well-documented scientific principles can give athletes a significant performance enhancement in hot environments. It is important to recognize the effect of acclimation on the tapering period, and plan accordingly.

William Henderson, MD, FRCPC, is a critical care physician and exercise physiologist who provides coaching and exercise physiology testing services. He placed 51st at the 2009 Marathon des Sables.

Tips for Beating the Heat

With or without acclimation, there are numerous ways you can beat the heat.

- First and foremost, stay hydrated with a proper balance of electrolytes.
- Wear light-colored clothing to limit the absorption of sunlight.
- Wear wicking fabrics to pull moisture away from your skin to the exterior of the fabric, where it can evaporate and cool you.
- In dry climates douse yourself in water whenever possible. This could mean pouring extra water from your hydration system or wiping down with a wet towel or sponge at an aid station.
- On extremely hot days, take a couple of minutes to submerge in a cool body of water to cool your core.
- Run in the shade when it's available.
- Put ice in your hydration system.
- Put ice or snow under your hat. (Yes, I've logged plenty of trail runs when it was hot, but there was still plenty of snow to be found in the mountains.)

Hot-Weather Ultra Tips

Jamie Donaldson

Hot weather brings ultrarunning to another level. Not only do you have to deal with the distance, you also have to deal with the environmental factors. I like that challenge because you never really know what is going to happen when you start a hot-weather race!

Pre-Race Tips

• Put your body in the conditions it will have to face in the race. If it's a hot race, train for the heat by running in the heat.

• Get your body so comfortable with being uncomfortable that it feels normal to you. I run in a 200-degree Fahrenheit sauna (work up to one hour in it) for six weeks prior to the Badwater Ultramarathon. At first I can barely handle 10 minutes; by the end my body can handle an hour with no problems. This makes the conditions at Badwater feel cool!

• Get your body use to fueling in the heat. Practice drinking a lot and fueling while in the hot environment.

• I run in the hottest part of the day in layers—the more uncomfortable, the better. That way when all those layers are off, it will feel "easy" to your body!

Race Day Tips

• Don't be afraid to alter your pacing plan for when the day is at its hottest. If you go out too fast when it's super hot, then it will take more effort from your body to keep running and keep cool. If you take it at a slower pace when it's super hot, your body can keep itself cooler easier while you continue running. When it's cooler, you will be able to push the pace back up.

• I drink a little bit more than normal each hour during

Badwater, all while trying to make sure my electrolytes stay in balance. I monitor my "output," too, to see that I am processing the liquids.

• When it's really sunny and hot, cover up your skin in white, loose clothing. Make sure you are constantly wetting the clothing. I also wear a Cool Off bandanna with ice and put ice in my hat.

Jamie Donaldson has won the Badwater Ultramarathon three times ('08–'10), while twice setting the course record ('08 and '10). She has won numerous other ultramarathons, set the American track 200-kilometer record, and been a US representative at the 24 Hour World Championships.

Heat Cramps, Heat Exhaustion, and Heatstroke*

As mentioned at the outset, heat can have deleterious effects on your health. Heat cramps and moderate heat exhaustion occur at most hot-weather ultras, but do not present any lasting danger. On the other hand, severe heat exhaustion and heatstroke are serious conditions; however, they occur with much less frequency. What follows is a very brief look at each of these conditions. Additional information is found at www.iRunFar.com/rfp/resources.

Heat cramps are muscle pains or spasms that usually occur in the arms, legs, or abdomen caused primarily by sweat loss. They can be treated with rehydration or regaining electrolyte balance as well as a reduction in activity and body temperature. Heat cramps can be a symptom of heat exhaustion.

Heat exhaustion is expressed in an array of symptoms, including heavy sweating, paleness, muscle cramps, tiredness, weakness, dizzi-

* The information for this section was obtained from the US Centers for Disease Control and Prevention.

ness, headache, nausea or vomiting, and fainting. Increased heart rate, low blood pressure, as well as fast, shallow breathing may also indicate heat exhaustion. Drinking cold beverages, resting, and applying cold water to the body cool a person suffering from heat exhaustion. If the symptoms are severe or last for more than an hour, seek medical attention.

Heatstroke, which occurs when the body can no longer control its temperature, is the most serious of the heat illnesses. It can lead to permanent health complications and death. With heat exhaustion, the body stops sweating, which leads to a spike in body temperature, possibly up to 105 degrees F in just 10 to 15 minutes! Symptoms include an extremely high body temperature, red, hot, and dry skin with no sweat, a strong, rapid pulse, a throbbing headache, dizziness, nausea, confusion, and unconsciousness. In the case of heatstroke, contact emergency services immediately. Next, take the victim to a shady area and cool the victim as rapidly as possible. Place him or her in a body of cool water, if possible. As an alternative in dry climates, place the victim in light clothes or a light sheet doused in water for evaporative cooling.

Avoid Being Low at High Altitude

Ultrarunning calendars are filled with high alpine races just begging to be run. The problem? Most people live within a few thousand feet of sea level, which means their bodies are not acclimated to high altitude. As with heat, running at high altitude without acclimation can affect both health and performance. The body and, in particular, the cardiovascular system undergo a multitude of changes when presented with significant increases in altitude. We'll only look into those changes that are most relevant to a lowland runner ascending to moderate to high altitudes (7,000 to 14,000 feet) to run an ultramarathon. This section looks at some of the body's adaptations to high altitude, issues faced when arriving at altitude, and rare but serious health complications that can arise at high altitudes.

High altitude shouldn't stop you from running.
Just know how to stay safe. (Photo by author)

The Effects of Altitude

Hypoxia, or lack of oxygen, is the primary reason for performance degradation at altitude. The amount of oxygen in the atmosphere decreases logarithmically with increases in altitude. This means that aerobic performance, which is oxygen-dependent, is unaffected below 3,000 feet and minimally affected below 6,500 feet. Above 6,500 feet aerobic performance quickly worsens as altitude increases further. The impact of hypoxia also worsens as race length increases. Hence, running races like the Leadville 100-mile, which starts above 10,000 feet and tops out at 12,600, are an extreme challenge.

One the body's quickest adaptations to high altitude is a gradual increase in ventilation, the volume of air respired, over the course of hours and days of arrival. The increase in ventilation has a nearly linear relationship with arterial oxygen saturation, a measure that indicates how close blood is to being fully oxygenated. The more oxygenated your blood, the more that's available for your muscles. For a sea-level runner, the vast majority of ventilatory acclimation occurs within four days of ascending altitudes up to 10,000 feet. While there is a larger increase in resting ventilation than ventilation while exercising, the increase while exercising is significant (about 10 percent).

While improvement in resting oxygen saturation plateaus at around eight days, oxygen saturation during exercise continues to increase through three weeks of altitude acclimation. A multitude of adaptations make this possible despite ventilation having plateaued long ago.

In the first two or three days after arriving at altitude, your basal metabolic rate increases before returning to normal between one and three weeks after arrival. The basal metabolic rate is the body's energy expenditure and it makes up a majority of a non-exercising person's daily caloric needs. Because we can only sustain burning limited number of calories per hour during an ultramarathon, diverting some of these calories due to a small but significant increase in basal metabolic rate may decrease athletic performance.

For most people, an increase in red blood cell count is likely the first adaptation they think of when contemplating altitude acclimation. However, increased red blood cell count, which increases the ability to transport oxygen, is one of the body's slowest adaptations to altitude. For example, a lowlander traveling to 10,000 feet in Leadville, Colorado, would not experience an increase a change in red bloods within his or her first 10 days in town.

Arriving and Acclimating at Altitude

Ideally, you would arrive at altitude three or more weeks before competing in an event at or above 8,000 feet. However, to be realistic, you're likely to spend a week or less at race altitude prior to competing. With that in mind, it's important to determine when you should ideally arrive within the week prior to race day.

During the first week at altitude, minimizing the short-term ill effects of altitude is as important as performance-related acclimation, if not more so. In particular, acute mountain sickness (AMS) is common among lowlanders arriving at moderate elevation (as low as 6,500 feet) and more acclimated individuals ascending thousands of feet above the altitude to which they're acclimated. Given the altitudes of ultras in the North America and Europe, the vast majority of AMS cases will be unpleasant, but nothing more. Symptoms can include headache, difficulty sleeping, drowsiness, dizziness and lightheadedness, fatigue, loss off appetite, nausea or vomiting, rapid heart rate, and shortness of breath during exertion. Or, as one book has put it, AMS resembles a case of "flu, carbon monoxide poisoning, or a hangover."* These symptoms can occur at any time after arriving at altitude, not just while running. The symptoms of AMS can present themselves within a few hours of ascent, but often on the second or third day at altitude. Symptoms typically subside within a day or two of onset. If you or someone you're with develops an extremely severe headache or vomiting that's not directly attributable to an aspect of ultrarunning, carefully monitor for other symptoms of high-altitude cerebral edema described below.

Be aware that a previous lack of AMS at a given altitude does not mean it won't occur the next time you're at that altitude. I've generally fared well in ascending to high altitude, but in the summer of 2009 I traveled to 10,000 feet in Leadville while acclimated to 6,000 to 7,000 feet and was still greeted by the worst headache of my life the day after my arrival.

With the effects of AMS in mind, those who can't manage an acclimation period of more than a week are best off arriving four or more days before the event. If that's not possible, arrive at altitude as close as possible to the start of the event to limit the onset of AMS and short-term performance decreases due to the initiation of acclimation.

* The Mountaineers. *Mountaineering: The Freedom of the Hills,* seventh edition. Seattle: Mountaineers Books, 2003.

Whenever you arrive at altitude, you are likely to experience a decrease in thirst and appetite. Therefore, upon arrival and in the days leading up to a race, drink more than usual to ensure you are properly hydrated. Those arriving from humid climes should keep in mind that sweat quickly evaporates in high, often dry climates. Don't let sweat (or thirst) dictate whether you need to drink before, during, or after your race. Since you'll also be less hungry at high altitude, eat according to your lowland habits as race day approaches. However, take in an extra 100 to 200 calories from carbohydrates per day, especially in the first few days at altitude. Carbohydrates are the body's favored energy source at altitude. Consuming them can keep you fueled as race day approaches and fend off possible dramatic weight loss.

When running at high altitude, protect yourself from increased exposure to ultraviolet (UV) radiation by wearing protective clothing, including a hat, and applying sunscreen. UV exposure, which can damage the skin and eyes, increases with altitude; if present, snow cover will reflect the UV radiation to further amplify its effects. UV exposure peaks at midday, not at the hottest time of day, so protect yourself in late-morning hours. Sunburn can occur in cold temperatures and under cloud cover. Do not wait for symptoms of sunburn to develop before taking precautions, as effects can lag exposure by up to a day.

High Altitude Pulmonary Edema and High Altitude Cerebral Edema

High altitude pulmonary edema (HAPE) and high altitude cerebral edema (HACE) are rare but potentially life-threatening conditions. Serious forms of the conditions are unlikely below 10,000 feet. It is extremely rare for an ultramarathon to expose a runner to a high enough altitude for a long enough duration to trigger either condition. Both conditions are preventable as they are preceded by recognizable symptoms, the recognition of which warrants returning to lower elevations immediately. To reiterate the last point, do not stop on the top of a mountain to rest or wait out the symptoms of HAPE or HACE—descend immediately!

If this were a book on high-altitude mountaineering, these subjects would warrant an entire chapter regarding recognition and treatment; however, in the context of ultramarathons there are but three pieces of advice: Recognize the symptoms of HAPE and HACE, respect their seriousness, and remove the affected person to lower altitude as quickly as possible.

HAPE is the accumulation of fluid in the lungs. It is typically diagnosed by the occurrence of at least two of the following symptoms—difficulty of breathing at rest, cough, weakness or decreased exercise performance, and chest tightness or congestion—as well as at least two of the following signs: crackles or wheezing in at least one lung, blue skin coloration, rapid shallow breathing, and rapid heart rate. Having paced at the Hardrock 100, which includes seven 13,000-plus-foot passes, I've seen a runner turn around while climbing the final pass 85 miles into the race out of respect for the HAPE symptoms he was experiencing.

HACE, the rarer of the two conditions, begins as AMS and progresses as brain tissue leaks fluids, leading to swelling. Symptoms include those of AMS with the addition of confusion, changed behavior, difficulty speaking, hallucinations, blindness, limb paralysis, seizure, unconsciousness, total paralysis, or coma. One simple test for HACE is to see if person in question can walk in a straight line; an inability to do so indicates HACE.

Chill Out with Cold-Weather Running

Although a few ultras are run in extremely cold conditions, they're much rarer than hot or high altitude ultras. As such, this section talks about the moderately cold conditions that most of us face in training and racing.

In cold weather, the saying "There's no such thing as bad weather, just bad clothing" holds true. (Photo courtesy of Nick Yardley)

Clothing

As suggested in chapter 7's "Staying Safe on the Trails," clothing is a runner's shelter. While this book won't give a full winter wardrobe lesson, there are some general points to keep in mind when dressing for the cold. To start, dress in layers that let you adjust your temperature so that you're never too hot or too cold. Being too hot is a serious problem—you'll sweat, get your clothing wet, and be in trouble if you start cooling off. I find that layers with zippers, such as a half-zip tech tee, provide for temperature micromanagement. When you're choosing layers, bring one more than you'll need in case you slow down or temperatures drop. Often, you'll start with that extra layer on until you warm up. Anticipate and put on appropriate clothing before you get cold. It's much harder to rewarm yourself than it is to stay warm in the first place. One last word on winter clothing: Leave the cotton at home. Cotton is a horrible insulator when wet, which happens easily enough via sweat when you're running.

Hydration, Fueling, and Other Tasks

Freezing temperatures make hydration problematic. For example, it's not uncommon for a water bottle valve or hydration pack hose to freeze. Sometimes you can break up the ice, but it's better to prevent it from freezing in the first place. If you've ever seen rock salt spread on a road, then you've observed electrolytes lower the freezing point of water to make it liquid at lower temperatures. The same thing happens when you add electrolytes to your running beverage. If adding electrolytes doesn't do the trick, fill your hydration system with warm or even hot water. Insulation accessories are available for many hydration packs, their hoses, and water bottles. There are even some sports water bottles with built-in insulation. In extremely cold weather, wear a hydration pack under your jacket while routing the hose up through the collar opening. For those carrying a bottle, try carrying it upside down (if it doesn't leak), as ice will form first on the top of the fluid, leaving the valve functional. Whatever your setup, take small frequent sips and blow any excess water out of a bottle's valve or hydration pack hose to prevent total freeze-up.

Low temperatures can put a damper on eating as well. In the cold, easily squeezed energy gels turn into viscous messes, normally soft energy chews can take out a tooth, and energy bars can become unbreakable super materials. To solve the problem of cold food, either bring food that's less susceptible to the cold or keep your food warm. On the latter point, you can store you food inside a jacket or in a pocket that sits against your body. You can also simply hold the desired delectable in your hand for a couple of minutes before consuming it. Whether from wearing gloves or cold fingers, the cold can make it difficult to access wrapped food. Prepare your food by making a small starter incision or choose food that's easily opened.

Cold or gloved hands can make any task more difficult. Avoid situations that will require fine finger movement. Should your hands become moderately cold, try balling them up. If that doesn't work, put them in a body nook, such as an armpit, under your clothing.

Traction

If you've run through a winter with snow and ice, you've experienced the slow and dangerous conditions they present. Perhaps you've already experimented with various ways to improve your traction in slippery circumstances. Regardless, you can investigate a number of winter running traction options at www.iRunFar.com/rfp/resources.

Learning to Run in Cold Weather

If you're unfamiliar with cold-weather running, it's best to experiment safely. Don't go jumping off the treadmill and going for a 20-mile wilderness run in subzero temperatures. Instead start by testing your clothing and gear close to civilization until you are confident it works.

Hypothermia, Frostnip, and Frostbite*

If you dress properly and take care of yourself, you can safely run in mind-numbingly cold temperatures. However, you can run into cold-related danger even in temperatures that are well above freezing.

Given enough exposure, hypothermia can set in even under temperate conditions. Hypothermia occurs when the body loses heat more quickly than the body produces it, leading to a decrease in body temperature. For a runner, this typically means prolonged exposure to cold without adequate clothing. Getting wet, whether from precipitation, a body of water, or sweat, increases the chances of hypothermia. Unblocked wind also exacerbates heat loss. Hypothermia is especially a concern among trail runners, as regard-

* Much of the information for this subsection was gathered from the Mayo Clinic website, www.mayoclinic.com.

less of season an injury in the backcountry can quickly turn a warmth-generating run into a cold slog or survival huddle. This is why trail runners must be prepared to withstand a few hours unmoving in any conditions they may face.

On the medical side, a person is technically hypothermic once their normal 98.6-degree Fahrenheit body temperature decreases to 95 degrees. Signs of hypothermia are shivering, clumsiness or lack of coordination, slurred speech or mumbling, stumbling, confusion or difficulty thinking, poor decision making (for instance, removing warm clothes), drowsiness or low energy, apathy about one's condition, progressive loss of consciousness, weak pulse, and shallow breathing. One particular danger of hypothermia is that you are unlikely to be aware of it. That makes it all the more important to deal with cold before or as soon as it comes on. If you encounter someone else with the signs of hypothermia, attempt to warm them and seek emergency medical assistance, if available.

When temperatures fall below freezing, frostbite becomes a concern. Frostbite is the freezing of the skin and the tissue beneath it. It typically occurs on exposed skin and smaller body parts, such as the fingers, toes, nose, ears, cheek, and chin. As frostbite approaches, the affected area becomes cold and then numb before turning hard and pale. Frostnip, a precursor to frostbite, occurs when the skin is irritated, but there is no permanent damage. Frostnip and mild frostbite can be treated by slowly warming the affected area with warm water. Severe frostbite requires medical attention to prevent serious complications.

14

THE ULTRARUNNING COMMUNITY

The ultramarathon community is both the best source of information about ultramarathons and one of the best reasons to engage in the sport. Embrace it. This chapter explains some ways to tap into that community before suggesting ways to share your experience with others.

Join the Ranks

One-on-one advice from ultrarunners is invaluable. Got friends who've run an ultra? Join them for one or many long runs and learn from them. Don't know any ultrarunners? Well, if you're part of a running club, ask around. You're likely to find one. Go run with him or her. If you know a few ultrarunners, try to learn from both the wily old veterans and the young bucks.

Want to up your ultra exposure? Find an ultrarunning club. There are plenty of them out there. Some ultra clubs are self-identified, such as the Chicago Ultrarunners (CHUGS) and St. Louis Ultrarunners Group (SLUGs). Identifying other ultra clubs isn't as straightforward. Having the word *trail* in a running club's name is a good sign that it's an ultra club in hiding. For instance, I came to ultras after finding the Virginia Happy Trails Running Club with its legions of ultrarunners. Finally, a number of road running clubs have ultra-running groups that rival many dedicated ultra clubs in terms of size and ambition. Given that it's not always easy to determine where ultra clubs exist, I've put together a directory of clubs, which can be found at www.iRunFar.com/rfp/resources/clubs.

A "trail running club" introduced me to and educated me about ultrarunning . (Photo courtesy of author)

There's much to be gained from running with an ultra club or its de facto counterparts. As mentioned above, learn from talking with experienced ultrarunners. There are few better ways to do this than by joining up with an ultra club. With an ultra club, you gain a slew of potential partners for your long training runs. Chances are you will find others training for similar-distance focus races around the same time as yours.

Your new ultra club may host "fat ass" events. These low-key, lightly supported non-races (described more fully at the outset of chapter 1) serve as great training runs. Often tailored more as social runs than competitive events, many fat asses include shorter options to increase participation. With that in mind, if a particular fat ass event fits well in your training schedule, but the distance is a bit too long, don't be afraid to check in with the run's organizer to learn about less-than-full-distance routes.

Call for Feedback on and Supplements to *Relentless Forward Progress*

We can all learn something from one another. That's why, as this book wraps up, I'm calling for your feedback. Please take the time to send me an email at:

relentlessforwardprogress@gmail.com

letting me know what you liked about the book and what you felt was lacking. Was there too much information on a subject or not enough on another? Were you left with any questions the book never answered?

Not only will your thoughts help me learn, but you may help other readers, as I will publish supplements to *Relentless Forward Progress* on iRunFar.com based on reader feedback. You can find them at www.iRunFar.com/rfp/resources. For more immediate answers to your ultrarunning questions, direct them to the entire iRunFar community at www.iRunFar.com/forum.

Ultrarunning and the Internet

While it's great to learn about ultrarunning directly from those around you, the Internet provides a nearly limitless set of ultrarunning resources and encouragement. You can find training plans for specific races, injury information, race description and reports, training tips, gear reviews, and many other information sources. If you're interested in seeing how the elites train, many share their training logs and running journals on the Web. For every elite blog, there are many middle- and back-of-the-packers sharing their personal running journeys on the net. You might better relate to the training volumes and concerns of these runners, so their blogs are worth checking out. What's more, connecting with other runners via blogs, ultrarunning forums, and email listservs provides you with a ready source of encouragement and reassurance when those in your everyday life might think you're crazy. Given that the Internet is so dynamic, a list of useful websites, blogs, and additional online resources will be maintained at www.iRunFar.com/rfp/resources.

At its core, ultrarunning is an individual sport. Training requires many hours spent out on the roads or trails. You might enjoy this solitude; however, it is enjoyable to share your experiences and connect with other like-minded runners. The good news is that it's easy to do so even away from races and running clubs. Blogs and social media allow even the least tech-savvy among us to embrace a community of runners around the world.

My own running-related writing career began by starting a personal running blog, like so many thousands of others. I found that I was able to easily share my running with my family and my running buddies. Over time, I connected with other ultrarunners. They gave me support and feedback regarding my running on my blog, while I returned the favor on their blogs as well. Those relationships further grew in online forums before resulting in in-person meetings and friendships. Although I belonged to both a road and a trail running club at the time, I could rarely meet up with those runners more than once a week. My small online running community kept me fired up the rest of the time.

Ultrarunning as a Family Affair

What about your own family and close friends? Unless they're runners, every time you head out for a run, you're spending time away from them. That's time away from helping with housework, running errands, watching the kids, or spending quality time with loved ones. The point of this is not to make you feel guilty; rather, it's to remind you that your own family makes many sacrifices to accommodate your ultra training and racing.

Including your family and friends in your ultrarunning puts a smile on their faces and yours. (Photo by Seppo Hinkula)

Sure, you might be conscientious to make sure you pick up the slack around the house or to spend extra quality time with them outside of training. However, consider ways to include friends and family in your training and racing. Ask them if they'd like to support you on a training run or at a race. You'd be surprised at how often your loved ones want to be part of your ultrarunning undertaking. They'll know that you want to spend time with them even when you are training and racing. In addition, they'll feel like they are a part of your training and accomplishments. You might even ask active family members to be pacers. (Many a family member has been converted to ultrarunning by way of pacing.) These and other efforts keep your non-running-related relationships happy and healthy, which often creates a feedback loop that funnels positive energy back into your running. As a bonus, you will probably have more fun, too!

Conclusion

Ultramarathons are a personal journey, but sharing that journey with others enhances it. I've learned much of the information contained in this book through countless conversations over many years. More recently, I've come to spend a good deal of my time sharing with others what I've learned about running ultramarathons. It's through this sharing, including writing this book, that I continue to learn from others about the sport on a continual basis. I encourage you to learn, share, and grow with those around you.

Happy trails,
Bryon

AFTERWORD: THE SKY IS NO LIMIT

Meghan M. Hicks

Becoming an ultrarunner is like graduating from superhero school. If you're certain that mainstream society has amply inquired about your marathon running habits, then wait until you experience their ultrarunning commentary. While compliments from family, friends, or co-workers are inherently uplifting, your champion status runs deeper than their perception. Once you've run an ultramarathon, you really *are* a superhero.

Running for 5, 12, or 24 hours during an ultramarathon requires an exquisite level of physical and mental fitness. In addition to racing, many runners deploy their wicked athleticism in innumerate other endurance adventures. Adventure runs, endurance snowshoeing, fastpacking, and stage racing are a few avenues to which you may apply your newfound superpowers.

Borrowing a term from road cycling, I call this stuff beyond-category adventuring. In cycling, beyond-category climbs are the toughest in terms of their combination of elevation gain and length. While some of this afterword's adventures are similarly rigorous, I call them beyond category for the way we use our physical and mental fitness to go beyond, into the infinity of possibility.

Being über-fit just plain feels good, but for me there's more to it. Said fitness allows me to explore some of our planet's awesome nooks and crannies. I recently found myself, while on a fastpacking trip through California's Sierra Nevada Mountains, on a 12,000-foot mountain pass. Up that high, it felt as if we were more in the heavens than on earth. That mountain pass is a metaphor for these beyond-category adventures: The sky is not even close to the limit.

Get Yer Adventure On

If you're like me, you've probably found yourself staring at an expanse of landscape, a far-off ridgeline, or a squiggling dirt road and thinking, *I want to go there.* If so, I have some grand news: As an ultrarunner, you probably can!

Some ultrarunners I know find inspiration for adventure runs in what's around them in their everyday worlds. Many endurance runners have, for example, laced their shoes and run from their town to the next one, simply because they wondered what it would be like to run a distance they usually drive. Other adventure runs may be big link-ups, connecting a series of ridges or valleys surrounding your hometown so that you can see them all in the course of one day. Some adventure runners I know vacation to a national park, lash food and water to their backs, and undertake an all-day expedition. Simply said, adventure runs provide an intimate and often surprising look at an old haunt or a new destination.

Ultrarunners are sometimes a competitive lot. Of the folks who take on trail adventure runs, some enjoy putting down fast times, known by the community as "fastest known times" or FKTs, during those runs. The speediest of adventure runners track FKTs via a forum hosted by ultrarunner Peter Bakwin. (Find a link to the FKT forum and other afterword-related resources at www.iRunFar.com/rfp/resources.)

One particularly popular adventure run is the Grand Canyon Rim-to-Rim-to-Rim, or R2R2R. Runners start at one of the Grand Canyon's rims, most often the South Rim, descend to the Colorado River at the canyon's bottom, climb to the far rim, then around, and run back to the rim on which they started. Though the Grand Canyon has many trails over which you can run R2R2R, the FKT was set using the South and North Kaibab Trails by ultrarunner Dave Mackey in 2007. Mackey covered this adventure run, which spans 42 trail miles and includes 10,000 feet of both elevation gain and descent, in less than seven hours!

At heart, I'm an adventurer, feeling pretty certain that I was put on this earth to dig my heels deep in some of our planet's wildest places. As such, I love a good adventure run. I adore this concept so much that, in 2006, my second ultradistance run was the Grand Canyon R2R2R. Running so many miles on legs that weren't acclimated to ultradistance travel disabled me for days with muscle soreness. However, a full day of running back and forth across one of the world's deepest canyons while observing its shifting shadows and moods made the discomfort more than worthwhile.

By Snowshoes We Endure

Most runners of our earth's temperate latitudes have experienced the challenge of training during the frigid and slippery winter. When training on the road, we sometimes slip-slide our way through an otherwise decent workout. On the coldest of winter days, we lament the peg-legged feeling that results from never quite warming up. And trail runners tuck their tails after the first snowstorm that buries their prized possessions, the trails, until next spring.

Snowshoes open up winter wonderlands. (Photo by author)

Have no fear. If you dislike winter running or if want an addition to it, endurance snowshoeing could be your answer. In my mind, snowshoeing is a perfect winter parley. It's superb cross training, requiring the use of little-employed-by-running muscles. Snowshoeing allows you play on snow-covered trails. And it's ample hard work, so you're sure to maintain, if not enhance, your fitness.

Endurance snowshoeing's crowning jewel is its simplicity. It's just you, your snowshoes, and the Wild West (or East, or North, or, on a stormy winter's day, the South). That is, the wilderness is your oyster. Get to know the winter side of all those trails you use so much during the summer!

Numerous companies manufacture a multitude of snowshoe models. Some are designed for running on groomed surfaces, while others are made for floating over deep powder. My recommendation: Buy a high-quality pair of snowshoes created for versatility. Other than snowshoes, all you need is a pair of waterproof and insulating shoes or boots, as well as some knee-high, waterproof gaiters.

Fit folks who take to endurance snowshoeing will likely find it to be a bit harder than normal hiking, but easier than running. However, if you find yourself moving through powder, the workout can turn anaerobic. As an ultrarunner, you'll quickly see what the fuss of endurance snowshoeing is all about: going as far as you'd like on top of the snow. Endurance snowshoeing is a magic-carpet ride to a whole new world of winter play.

Spend any time on a pair of snowshoes, and you'll likely notice that your rate of forward movement decreases by one leap and a few bounds. Movement in the supranivean world is often slower, harder work. For example, last year I set out on a backcountry snowshoeing trip with another fit ultrarunner and, despite our daily hard work, we mucked through about 30 miles of snowshoeing in four days' time.

One last note: Endurance snowshoeing can certainly last for more than one day. For example, I recently undertook a three-day outing. We spent each day on top of the snow and two nights in small, backcountry cabins.

Fastpack It

Begin with backpacking, a sport in which you hike trails and live out of a pack on your back for two or more days. Then halve your pack's volume and weight by removing most of the excess, luxury items. Don't forget to double your daily mileage plan. Instead of hiking 10 miles each day, let's shoot for 20. The result is fastpacking, the art of light and far foot travel through wild places that, among outdoor enthusiasts and especially trail runners, is experiencing a raging growth in popularity.

As the sport evolves, so does the range of appropriate equipment

Fastpacking is your express ticket to backcountry camping.
(Photo by author)

from which fastpackers can outfit themselves. Many gear companies now manufacture ultralight running backpacks, the lightest-of-light tents and sleeping bags, as well as cook stoves that weigh just a few dozen grams. Putting the latest and greatest gear on your back for a fastpacking trip isn't necessary, but you won't travel far unless you pare down your pack to the bare minimum.

Most fastpackers spend a goodly portion of the daylight hours on the trail in a mix of powerhiking and running. For example, on steep, uphill climbs, fastpackers powerhike, while the flats and downhill sections are perfect for a decent running clip. Come late afternoon fastpackers empty their packs, then set up the ultralight tents, sleeping bags, and cooking paraphernalia with which they recover from the day's work.

Fastpacking variants exist, like running with a small pack between established nightly dwellings, such as huts, yurts, or cabins. Hut-to-hut fastpacking is exceedingly popular in the Swiss Alps, for example, where a well-established trail network and perfectly spaced huts provide fastpackers and other backcountry users a warm space to bed down for the night.

Supported, multiday running is another variant of fastpacking. One summer, for example, a Canadian ultrarunner organized a five-day run across Banff National Park for a small group of her friends. By day the group ran, with the end point of one day being the next day's starting point. By night, instead of camping out in the bush, the group returned to the Canadian runner's home for good times, great food, and comfortable sleeping quarters.

Stage Races and the Art of Attrition

As if running one ultramarathon isn't enough, some ultrarunners run stage races, events lasting for multiple days with set distances to run each day punctuated by evenings of non-running recovery. Picture the Tour de France, the famous cycling stage race, then convert the race layout to running. Dozens of stage races exist with at least one on every continent, including Antarctica. Yes, should you have the burning (or, should I say, freezing) desire, you may enter a week-long race across a piece of the Antarctic continent.

Let's look at a hypothetical six-day stage race typical of many taking place around the world. In this example, runners race each day for six days to cover a total distance of about 150 miles. Most of the running days are roughly 20 miles in length, with two being at a marathon or ultramarathon distance. Between each racing stage, runners camp in simple dwellings and spend their time sleeping, eating, enjoying social time with other runners, and otherwise recovering.

With this magnifying-lens exam, the key to success fast emerges: taking care of yourself all week so that you aren't a victim of attrition. Stage racers must set a sustainable running pace for multiple days. Outrunning a certain competitor or time goal early in the week, for example, might leave you with leaden legs later on. Gearing your nutrition toward a week of effort is another critical aspect of success. While you may eat little to nothing during a single 20-mile race, stage racers eat more during a stage of the same length so as to keep their glycogen stores above empty all week. Thus, the victors of a stage race are the men and women who run the fastest while best managing the variables of racing, nutrition, hydration, foot care, sleep, weather, and whatever else the race throws their way.

I think this is precisely why many ultrarunners love stage races: Even though each day of the race isn't necessarily an ultramarathon distance, ultramarathons and stage races both require the management of a number of changing variables. Ultrarunners find these races attractive, too, because they travel through some of the same exotic places and trails as ultramarathons. Simply put, we ultrarunners are attracted to the challenging and the beautiful.

I'm a stage-racing fiend. In my five years of ultrarunning, I've completed four stage races in three different countries. While I've only sampled the world's buffet of these races, my hands-down favorite is Morocco's Marathon des Sables. In this race, nearly 1,000 competitors from more than 80 countries gather in the northern reaches of the Sahara Desert to run 150 miles over the course of seven days. Between days of racing, competitors live in an immense, nomadic race camp. At the end of the week, the competitor with the lowest cumulative time for the racing days becomes the winner.

I am often asked why I love MdS, as the race is known. I have no singular answer. Morocco possesses a charming, if unusual, culture. The orange sands of the Sahara Desert are beautiful enough to have their own siren call. Running with a massive group of runners from every end of our earth is invigorating. And the challenge of plying my body and mind to stay healthy for day upon day of racing is a fun one.

Dream It, Do It

If you haven't figured out the root of this ultrarunning business quite yet, I'm about to let you in on the sport's secret. *Happiness.* Simple, isn't it?

Many ultrarunners are driven, in part, by competition, by setting and achieving goals, or by spending time in attractive natural settings. But each of those motivations can be traced back to that secret: doing stuff that makes you happy.

So get out there and dream big and beyond category, all right?

Meghan M. Hicks is an adventurer who transitioned from the worlds of track, cross-country, and, later, marathons to ultramarathons, adventure runs, and stage races. She finished second female at the 2009 Marathon des Sables. As a writer and outdoor educator, Meghan highlights the close connections among people, place, and physical activity on her website, www.MeghanMHicks.com, in national publications, and in national parks.

APPENDIX:
BAREFOOT RUNNING
AND ULTRAMARATHONS

Michael Sandler and Jessica Lee

Ultradistance running can be one of the most enjoyable experiences on earth. Learn to run light and free and you'll find yourself running in the zone, effortlessly clicking off mile after mile, seeming to glide above the trails with your feet barely touching the ground.

I've been a long-distance runner and ultra-endurance athlete for many years. In addition to spending a summer camping out at almost 13,000 feet in Leadville, Colorado, to run all of her trails, I spent years trying to tick off every trail in the Pikes Peak region (preferably near or above tree line) before moving to northern Colorado. There I used Ironman training as an excuse to run everything I could in Rocky Mountain National Park and other alpine regions, typically with 8-to-10-hour runs.

I'm no stranger to long-distance events; in fact, you could call me an addict. To me, there's nothing better than heading out my backyard for an 8-to-12-hour "run around the block," as I like to call my adventures, except, of course, doing the same thing more than 11,000 feet above sea level. There's something magical to me about running above the tree line.

After my near-death accident five years ago, I was told I would never run again. I have a titanium femur, titanium hip, I've had 10 knee operations, I have almost no lateral or medial meniscus, no left ACL, and an inch leg-length discrepancy. And that's not to mention my condition as "Mr. Plantar Fasciitis" or "Mr. Flat Foot" as podiatrists, orthopods, and other medical specialists used to call me.

Doctors were right, I couldn't run again, until I began running barefoot. I started with only a couple hundred yards, running up light on my forefoot (as if I were running uphill) and then working on foot-strengthening exercises on the way back. Feeling the ground, something special happened: My feet grew strong and I found an extra-light stride, one that didn't stress my joints. I found a way to get balanced and to heal.

Through barefoot running I healed to where I'm once again running "around the block" silly distances, but this time with less effort and fatigue than ever before. My feet have gotten stronger—as podiatrists said, "I grew an arch." And by running barefoot, I've tapped into the energy and technique of indigenous people of the past, people who ran without shoes, or without modern shoes, longer and farther than we may ever run.

No matter the distance, desire, or terrain on which you train, if you want to run far, stay healthy, get strong, and run free, then you can benefit from barefoot running and barefoot training.

How Does Barefoot Running Help?

First, when you run barefoot, you're running awarefoot. That means you're waking up all the nerve endings on the bottom of your feet. This helps you when you're barefoot to discover your lightest stride possible, which you'll carry back into your shoe. It also helps you develop the vestibular system (balance mechanism) of the body, helping you run better on uneven terrain and surfaces, run with less chance of falling, or of rolling or twisting an ankle. The more we wake up this awareness, the more we dance, rather than trod along the trails. A 100-mile dance with nature sounds much better than a 100-mile slog, now doesn't it?

Second, when you run barefoot, you quickly find heel striking to be a big no-no. The first time you hit your heel on the ground barefoot, you stop, or go home. In 2009 Dr. Daniel Lieberman of Harvard University published a study that found runners hit the ground on average three times harder in a shoe than out of a shoe, and with an initial impact force, or impact transient (shock wave), that's virtually non-existent out of a shoe.

Why's that? Because when we're out of a shoe we tend to land on our forefoot, using the entire foot and leg, from our bow-shaped metatarsals, to our arches (which can grow quite strong) to our Achilles tendon (the only tendon capable of holding 2,000 pounds of force) to our calves, quads, hamstrings, and glutes as a fantastic 2-to-3-foot-long shock absorber or spring-like mechanism. Strengthen the spring, lean forward slightly as you run (without bending at the waist), and gravity does the work of carrying you forward. Conversely, land with your heels, or even midfoot, and something dramatically different happens. The foot and leg no longer act as a spring and shock absorber, but instead as a transmitter of impact. With each step we hit the brakes, robbing ourselves of valuable kinetic energy, and instead send a shock wave straight up through our feet, legs, knees, hips, into our backs, and up through our shoulders and our necks.

If we want to run light, or to run like the Kenyans, Ethiopians, or Tarahumara, then we need to learn how to land on our forefoot—something barefoot running naturally promotes. Once we learn this technique, we can carry it back into a shoe, although chances are we'll use a slightly different one, one that's closer to the ground, doesn't have a high heel to throw off our center of gravity or how we hit the ground, and that's more flexible and lets us "feel" the ground.

Baby-Step Your Way into Running Light and Free

With the recent explosion in popularity of barefoot running due to the runaway best seller *Born to Run*, it's tempting to just shed your shoes and go the distance barefoot. One would assume we'd be able to run light and fast like the Tarahumara, either in our minimalist huaraches, Vibram FiveFingers, or completely barefoot.

Unfortunately, this isn't quite true, at least for now.

While barefoot running or using a barefoot running technique has some tremendous advantages for ultradistance runners, it's something to tread into lightly and extremely slowly.

Barefoot running can help you run lighter, faster, farther, and more efficiently than ever before, and with less impact and less chance of injury. But it requires patience, diligence, and time to build into. Though you are born with the natural ability to run and with proper stride, it takes time for your body to relearn.

Whether you're working into minimalist footwear, or some fully barefoot running, you'll want to start fully barefoot to begin. (You can find more tips on transitioning at RunBare.com or in our book *Barefoot Running: How to Run Light and Free by Getting in Touch with the Earth*.)

Begin with only a few hundred yards, just enough to let your feet feel the ground and begin to wake up. You have more nerve endings on the bottoms of your feet than almost anywhere else in the human body—it's why you're feet are so ticklish and why reflexology exists. By going barefoot you're taking the blindfolds off your feet and letting them feel and sense the ground, finding your lightest stride possible.

Going fully barefoot lets your skin be your guide. It helps keep you from doing too much, something we're all too capable of doing as ultrarunners. Turns out the fitter we are and the more of a distance athlete we are, the more likely we are to overdo it. So go fully barefoot for the first few weeks, letting your skin stop you when it's tired. Carry your shoes with you as "handweights" and never be afraid to put them back on early if your skin tells you to.

You see, it's much better for your soft and sensitive skin to tell you to stop, rather than cooking the muscles, ligaments, tendons and even bones on the inside. So let your skin be your guide.

Getting into barefoot running or a barefoot running style takes time for several key reasons. First, our feet aren't used to moving three-dimensionally; they've been trapped and adapted to the world of a two-dimensional shoe. That means the twisting and rotating that a bare or nearly bare foot experiences is more than it's used to. Second, the foot, calf, and Achilles are all weak and atrophied. The muscles of the feet take time to build back (the great news is you *can* grow an arch, and you *can* strengthen those feet!), and your calves and Achilles, once stuck in shoes with a high heel, have to stretch, elongate, and slowly return to their natural length. (Your Achilles can shorten up to 50 percent in high-heeled shoes.) Check out your running shoes—they have higher heels than you thought! Additionally, barefoot running is running nice and light on your forefoot, which is the equivalent of doing a calf-raise with each and every stride. Picture doing 100 calf-raises a minute for the next 20 to 30 minutes. That's several thousand calf-raises for only a 5k. Picture what that'll do to you if you don't build in slowly. (If you're reading this, already own a pair of Vibrams, and didn't start slowly, then you *know* what I'm talking about!)

To transition safely, you'll need to start with very short distances and build up slowly. Increase 100 yards every other day, always "resting" (no barefoot time) on the in-between days. You can continue your normal runs with your traditional stride and distance. As your barefoot time builds up over time, cut back your traditional shod time accordingly. (I have a 3-times rule. Until you've fully adapted, 1 mile barefoot is the equivalent of 3 miles in a shoe.) Always do your barefoot time first, before your feet are hot and sweaty, and before your body fatigues. (Barefoot running is all about proper form, which trumps strength and endurance any day.) Then when you're back in your traditional shoe, go back to your old form for now (giving the muscles, ligaments, tendons, and bones a chance to recover and build back stronger). After approximately three months you can begin to transition your form in a shoe, too, but give this time; at first focus on the new stride *only* out of a shoe to let your skin be your guide.

There are some great advantages to learning barefoot running technique, though I'm not advising you go out, buy a pair of minimalist running shoes, and use them for your next ultra. Transitioning takes great time, and there's something to be said for the protection on the bottom of your feet. If you read *Born to Run* and remember the Tarahumara Indians (really called the Raramuri) winning the race, they were in huarache sandals made of retreaded tires . . . not exactly minimalist, to say the least! Your feet take time to adapt, and during that time must be protected from rocks and other obstacles underfoot. If not, you'll tear up your feet literally on the outside *and* on the inside.

With my book tour, I still run an average of 100-plus miles a week (sometimes much more), and though I'm more than four years into this game, my feet are still adapting. I'm fully barefoot for my short distances (10 to 20 miles on smooth terrain, 5 to 10 on really rocky terrain), and then start to add more and more shoe as the distances increase. I'll always want a shoe without a high heel (I don't want the bad form the heel promotes, nor the strain it puts on the body), and I'll always want a shoe with flexibility so I can feel the ground and move the foot naturally. But what I'll want as the distances increase is *protection*. Until my feet are harder than nails (and even the Tarahumara may wear shoes), I want something fairly substantial on the bottom of my feet if I'm going the distance.

Barefoot Benefits

So now that I've gone over the dos and don'ts, what are the benefits of going barefoot, or training barefoot as the case may be?

Indigenous people have been running barefoot or in sandals for thousands of years and are some of the best endurance athletes out there. First off, there are the modern-day Kenyans and Ethiopians, who all ran barefoot as children and regularly kick butt in everything from 1,500-meter track races through the marathon. They run with an amazing forefoot stride, gliding along as if they're in second gear and everyone else is still in first (which technically, by running that way, is the case). Then there are the legendary Tarahumara and other Native American tribes whose messengers have run 100-to-200-mile runs or longer in a single go, either fully barefoot or with just a sandal on their foot. Then there are the Incan and Aztec messengers, famous, too, for their 100-plus-mile jaunts. There are African messengers, Aborigine runners, Maori, Turkish messengers, Tibetan Lung-Gom-Pa runners, and even modern-day marathon monks of Mount Hiei in Japan, all of whom run with almost nothing on their feet and are said to glide effortlessly for hundreds of miles at a time.

How do they do it? And how can we benefit from their experience?

They do it, as previously mentioned, by running with more of a forefoot strike, in essence running in second gear. When you're barefoot, you quickly find that a heel strike hurts. Without a shoe to promote bad form, you quickly get off your heel and up onto your forefoot.

By learning to run barefoot, we not only reduce the impact on our bodies, instead turning our legs into natural springs, but gain far greater efficiency as well. When we're landing on our heels, and to a lesser extent our midfoot, we have to hit the brakes with every stride. This puts us in a constant game of braking and reaccelerating. It takes its toll on the body with constant eccentric muscle contractions (muscles having to lengthen at the same time they're trying to shorten; picture the sensation of running a long downhill and what it does to your quads, then remember that that's what you're doing with every stride in a traditional shoe), which gradually weaken our muscles and leave them a quivering wreck. It's also forcing us to work extra hard, wasting valuable energy we can ill afford to spend over the distance. In essence, we're fighting a law of physics as we run in our shoes: the law of conservation of momentum. Instead of conserving momentum, or what I like to refer to as "respecting King Mo," we destroy it with each and every step.

This is a big no-no in running for all distances, but particularly for *long* ones where the name of the game is conserving energy. For if you're fried and fatigued, then no matter how strong you are, you're goose is cooked (even if you're vegan).

Your future barefoot running stride is more efficient for two more key reasons. First, when you're running barefoot, or with a barefoot-like stride, your stride shortens as your stride rate increases. You go from a stride rate from as few as 110 strides per minute to more like 180, or about that of pedaling a bicycle. This helps further conserve momentum (less braking), reduces the work your legs have to do with each landing (running is really a controlled fall, and the shorter the distance we have to fall or land on each leg, the less work it has to do, and the less it'll be fatigued over the distance), and greatly reduces the up-and-down bouncing we do from stride to stride. In a traditional shoe we try to "stride out" or reach long between strides to maximize the cushioning of our shoes—in essence, to land on our heels. When we go barefoot and get off the heels, we bring the strides in closer and closer. (This again conserves your legs; it's like going into a smaller gear on a bicycle to get up a hill . . . less leg work, less leg fatigue.) Additionally, it means we don't have to leap up and down between strides to stride out or reach long.

Did you know the average runner bounces 3 inches up and down between strides? That doesn't sound like much, does it? But do you know what that is over the course of a marathon? That's a full vertical mile a runner's gone uphill at the same time he or she has run 26.2. Multiply that by nearly four for a 100-miler, and you've run over 20,000 feet into the sky, even on the flattest of course! Even worse, though, is it's 4 vertical miles you've come downhill onto your heel or foot, driving force up through the body. That's why we're so wrecked at the end: because we've been bouncing up and down, pounding our bodies over the distance. When you shorten your stride, you lessen the bounce. And when you train barefoot, you can feel yourself bouncing (going barefoot, or awarefoot, is really a game of awareness or shutting off the iPod and going inside your body to find your lightest stride), and work to eliminate it. Reduce your bounce by an inch, and you've eliminated one mountain on your course. Reduce it by another inch, and that's two fewer Pikes Peaks you have to climb in your race. See the difference?

Training barefoot helps you wake up the mind–body connection, find your lightest stride, and develop yourself into the most efficient runner you can be. It greatly reduces impact on your body, too, helping you to go the distance year after year. Finally, by feeling the ground, you gain greater proprioception (body sense over the ground), gaining the agility (becoming more nimble) that helps you to dance from rock to rock, keep from falling, or prevent rolling an ankle. And of course, as a longtime barefoot runner, I'd say it just feels great, too. There's something amazingly special about connecting with Mother Nature through the dirt beneath my feet, and truly being connected to the trail. When I'm barefoot, I'm no longer watching the scenery, but a part of it. I feel I draw power from the earth, power and strength that help me go the distance.

Less is more when it comes to running the distance; that's why great runners like Anthony Krupicka have been shaving the heels off their shoes for years. Just get into this slowly. Baby-step your way in with a little barefoot running, and very slow, incremental changes to your form and your footwear. As the Tortoise always said to the Hare, slow and steady wins the race. Have fun!

For more information on barefoot running including proper form, a step-by-step transition, overcoming the elements, minimalist footwear, injury prevention, healing, and recovery, check out Michael Sandler and Jessica Lee's best seller Barefoot Running: How to Run Light and Free by Getting in Touch with the Earth *at RunBare.com or join their RunBare Facebook page. Be well and run free!*

About the Author

Photo by Brightroom.com

Bryon Powell has loved trail running since going out for his high school cross country team in 1992. A decade later, his introduction to ultra-running gave him the ability to run his beloved trails nearly without end. By October 2007, he found himself increasingly drawn to informative writing on the subject, which led to his development of the trail running and ultramarathon website, iRunFar.com. This love blossomed, as well. In May 2009, Bryon left his job as a Washington, DC, attorney to dedicate himself full time to spreading the word about trail running and ultrarunning. His work has appeared in numerous national publications, including *Outside, Runner's World, Running Times, Trail Runner, Competitor Running*, and *UltraRunning*. He's also a contributing editor at *Trail Runner* and an advisory board member of the American Trail Running Association. In addition to writing, Bryon has coached many runners to their first ultra or first 100 finishes while helping others break course records at major ultramarathons. Needless to say, despite his writing and coaching, Bryon still runs ultras. He's twice placed in the top ten at the Leadville 100 ('06 & '09), twice won the under-30 age group at the Western States 100 ('04 & '05), and was part of the first American team to place in the top three at Morocco's Marathon des Sables ('09).

iRunFar.com

Want to learn about the people, places, gear, and races that make trail running and ultrarunning so exciting? Look no further than iRunFar.com. Published by Bryon Powell and a team of experts, it regularly provides:

★ In-depth reviews of shoes and other running gear
★ Race previews and post-race analysis
★ Live race day coverage
★ Interviews with top ultrarunners and trail runners
★ News and discussions on ultramarathoning's hot issues
★ Training and racing tips

iRunFar.com is also your supplement to *Relentless Forward Progress*. Find resources and updates to the book at: www.iRunFar.com/rfp/resources.

In addition, iRunFar.com is more than an online magazine, it's a community. In the comments on each article, you'll get insight from coaches, race directors, industry insiders, and elite ultrarunners, as well as runners like you! Use the iRunFar forums at www.iRunFar.com/forums to have your ultrarunning questions answered by the iRunFar staff and readers. The community and its conversations continue on iRunFar's Facebook page and Twitter feed.

Visit iRunFar and get involved today!

iRunFar.com
Mud, mountains, miles, and more

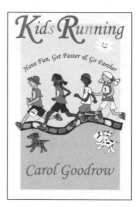

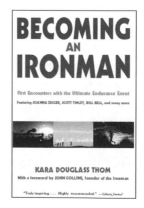

www.breakawaybooks.com

IN BOOKSTORES EVERYWHERE